HOPE

ON A STRANGE PLANET

HOPE

ON A STRANGE PLANET

CHAPLAIN STEPHEN DICKS

ARCHWAY
PUBLISHING

Archway Publishing books may be ordered through booksellers or by contacting:

Archway Publishing
1663 Liberty Drive
Bloomington, IN 47403
www.archwaypublishing.com
1 (888) 242-5904

Because of the dynamic nature of the Internet, any web addresses or links contained in this book may have changed since publication and may no longer be valid. The views expressed in this work are solely those of the author and do not necessarily reflect the views of the publisher, and the publisher hereby disclaims any responsibility for them.

Any people depicted in stock imagery provided by Thinkstock are models, and such images are being used for illustrative purposes only. Certain stock imagery © Thinkstock.

Scripture taken from the Holy Bible, NEW INTERNATIONAL VERSION®. Copyright © 1973, 1978, 1984 by Biblica, Inc. All rights reserved worldwide. Used by permission. NEW INTERNATIONAL VERSION® and NIV® are registered trademarks of Biblica, Inc. Use of either trademark for the offering of goods or services requires the prior written consent of Biblica US, Inc.

This book is a work of non-fiction. Unless otherwise noted, the author and the publisher make no explicit guarantees as to the accuracy of the information contained in this book and in some cases, names of people and places have been altered to protect their privacy.

ISBN: 978-1-4808-5136-8 (sc)
ISBN: 978-1-4808-5137-5 (hc)
ISBN: 978-1-4808-5135-1 (e)

Library of Congress Control Number: 2017953689

Print information available on the last page.

Archway Publishing rev. date: 9/28/2017

To the five greatest women in the entire world: Bonnie Hutchinson, Kay Bien, Melissa Bradshaw, Shirley Barnes, and most especially the love of my life and mother of my children, Jennifer Dicks. You have each invested in my life far more than I can ever hope to repay.

To the five greatest men in the entire world: Raymond Dicks, Lee Bien, Byron Barnes, Craig Fullerton, and Frank Hart. You each taught me what it means to be a man. In whatever I attempt, you have been the ones that I ask in my head, "Would it make you proud?"

To the four greatest brothers in the entire world: Robert Turner, Larry Turner, Adam Champion, and Brian Bradshaw. You each make me want to be a better man so I can be worthy of being called your brother.

To the four greatest children in the entire world: Ashley, Kaylee, Tina, and Stephen Dicks. As each of you prepare to make your mark on this world, know that you have already forever changed mine for the better. Thank you for granting me the greatest title I have ever achieved ... Dad.

To my adopted family: Bill and Janelle Colwell, Mark and Mike Bivins, Darryl Metcalf, John Green, Eddy Ford, Sandra Chugen, Camille Acred, Teresa Watson, Justin Cox, and Daniel

Cottingham. Thank you for letting me be family. My life is better for having been a part of yours.

To the brave men and women of our Armed Forces—past, present, and future: you make me proud to be an American and humbled to be numbered among your ranks.

ACKNOWLEDGMENTS

I wish to acknowledge my personal heroes: the men and women of the Armed Forces who time and time again have answered their nation's call to go into harm's way. Their selfless service, professionalism, compassion, and superhuman efforts make them the best fighting force in the entire world.

I would like to especially acknowledge the brave men and women whom I served alongside in Iraq in the 28th Combat Support Hospital (CSH) and the 40th Military Police Battalion. There are none better.

This compilation of my journal entries from two separate deployments would have remained in a cluttered drawer of personal memories had it not been for the encouragement and amazing editorial talents of my mother, Bonnie Hutchinson. Thank you for believing in me.

To the wonderful team at Archway Publishing from Simon & Schuster, thank you for choosing to accept my manuscript for publishing. I am sure my paying up front had very little to do with your decision.

Finally, I would like to ensure it is known, to whomever may read these pages, that the greatest source of inspiration in my life, the best parts of who I am, the wellspring of anything good that may come out of my existence is due first to my God and His Son, my Savior Jesus Christ. Secondly, it is due to the constant love and support of my wife and children, Jennifer, Ashley, Kaylee, Tina, and Stephen. I am so incredibly proud of each of you. You make my life worth living well.

Chaplain (LTC), ret Glenn C. Sammis, D.Min, LPC

Anyone who has ever donned a military uniform will appreciate the stark reality and the impassioned humor of *Hope On a Strange Planet*. This is especially true for those who have traveled to that "strange planet." Anyone who has loved and supported a military service member who has made that journey has experienced a change in lifestyle and a deep concern for the well-being of their loved one. In this book, they may gain new understanding of their loved one's sacrifice and they will also hear one Soldier's deep appreciation of the support from his family and loved ones. Chaplain Dicks speaks for most of us who have ever worn the uniform as he talks about how that love and support sustained him through the toughest of times. For those who have never been connected with the military, he brings an understanding of what life is like on a "strange planet" in a combat zone. For all readers Hope displays the character and values of "the real Soldier chaplain." Over 46 years of observing and living with and around Soldiers tells me that is what Soldiers need from their chaplain. Chaplain Dicks has broken the code of what his Soldiers need. His writing indicates what "the real Soldier chaplain" looks like, sounds like, and acts like.

In the years since the innovation of the all-volunteer Army, there has been a widening gap between how the American populace understands the American Soldier and how the American Soldier understands him/herself. An American Legion award winner, Dale Dye, has struggled with the Hollywood perception of the American fighting man/woman. He said that he was tired of the movie depiction of the American Veteran and the military not being portrayed in an accurate manner. He's right. It is true that often the public does not understand the mentality of the American Soldier. The Soldier is often vilified or romanticized. That is part of the difficulty in providing appropriate care for the Veterans who struggle with the emotional and spiritual difficulties that come with the combat experience. Chaplain Dicks gets it. Anyone who picks up this book and reads it can come away with a clear understanding of a Veteran.

Of late, there has been much interest in the term *resiliency* and what makes a person resilient. When you read *Hope*, you will find what has contributed to making Chaplain Dicks a picture of resiliency. The sharing of his story tells you he is a spiritual being with a sense of humor, a sense of purpose, and sense of optimism in the face of reality. He shares the hope portrayed by Victor Frankl, the Auschwitz concentration camp survivor. Hope is the one ingredient in life that we cannot live without. As Frankl indicates, we die when hope is gone. He would observe persons in the prison camps with him who lost hope. He would watch as they would lay down where they stood and died. When hope was gone life was gone. It is the role of the "Soldier chaplain" to bring hope in the midst of the chaos of war. Chaplain Dicks is such a "Soldier chaplain." There is certainly much in his book to give one hope. It is the hope that supports and saves lives that are present in the narrative of Chaplain Dicks. His presence communicates to his Soldiers that hope is present.

Chaplains often find themselves in the most intractable

situations. For some problems there is no good decision to be found. It is in those circumstances that the chaplain brings hope to the Soldiers who face those situations. It is also in those situations that the "Soldier chaplain" brings his/her faith. No real chaplain believes that they are a god in any situation. It is the real chaplain who understands that their presence offers the faith and hope that God is present in all situations. The chaos of war is one of the most significant challenges to the belief of the existence of God. It is the chaplain's presence that says clearly that God is alive and well in the presence of the most defined evil. It is clear that Chaplain Dicks understands the significance of the representation of hope. Hope is alive in the presence of the chaplain on the "distant planet." It is in the presence of belief and hope that the Soldier can find meaning in his/her chaotic world that includes death and destruction.

"Soldier chaplains" will sometimes refuse to display feelings that the chaplain believes would be seen as weakness. They want people to think them perfect, able to handle anything without anger, hurt, sadness, or any of the other feelings Soldiers think weak. It is not in perfection that the chaplain represents that hope. It is rather in his or her ability to be real that says that God is real and present. To pretend that one does not feel the pain, the fear, the terror, or the helplessness is to hide God's presence from the other Soldiers who feel those same things. It is the true concept of the wounded healer* that makes the chaplain the most effective purveyor of hope. Even to admit the sense of rage that comes with helplessness is the task of the chaplain. It is in being real, sharing his/her own experience, that the chaplain is empowered to relate to Soldiers (and to their Families). God's grace is present in that moment. In being a human being with human feelings and struggles the chaplain enables Soldiers to believe that hope is also real and that life has meaning. It is a renowned psychotherapist and author's rule for life that "Real is better than perfect." The Soldier is truly tested in the chaos of the combat zone. To pretend not to feel is to deny one's humanity. The research tells us that one's ability to express feeling is an important part of resilience. In sharing his life Chaplain Stephen Dicks reveals what is real and resilient. He is a role model for other chaplains and for other Soldiers who strive for that resilience. He is an example of one chaplain who finds meaning in his struggle. This engaging story is of a "Soldier-chaplain."

*The concept of the wounded healer was originated in the thinking of Carl Jung and developed for clergy in the writing of Henri Nouwen *(The Wounded Healer, 1979)*. The wounded healer presented in this situation is the chaplain who is aware of his own helplessness, suffering, fear, angst, anger, and other emotions that can be so difficult to resolve. She/he may encounter the same nightmares, hyperawareness, withdrawal, flash anger, and other experiences that often come with the facing of trauma. The wounded healer in this context is willing to face, consciously experience, and go through the wound to achieve and understand the greater meaning. She/he uses this experience to enable his/her ministry for the Soldiers who are his/her parish.

CONTENTS

JOURNEY TO ANOTHER PLANET

Millions upon millions of innocent people have gone off to war. I have never heard of anyone who returned innocent. I suppose there is always hope it could happen because hope is one of the "big three" mentioned in the Bible. You know, "faith, hope and love, but the greatest of these is love," from 1 Corinthians, chapter 13. That passage is normally read at weddings to assure the happy couple that their chances are better than average at beating the odds for divorce.

I'm a big believer in hope. I hope they make it as I say words like "forever" and "till death do you part." I try to ignore the nagging thought in the back of my head that keeps screaming, *Or until it's too inconvenient to put up with each other, and you decide to be unfaithful; you know, forever until then.* Pessimistic, I know, and I fight against it.

When my sarcasm mixes with the harshness of reality, it can either tip me to bitterness or wrap me in a protective blanket of humor that makes the difficult times more bearable. The strength of the hope I have in any given situation tends to be the deciding factor for which side I land on. You see, even when life and people disappoint, hope never does. Even if what you're hoping for doesn't actually pan out, you have a good run of positive anticipation for whatever it is, and that fact alone feels pretty good. Hope gives a great handhold on life, even in the sad times when your fingers ultimately get slammed in the proverbial door. In fact, if they do, with hope, you can instantly begin hoping the pain will go away. That little bit of light helps in facing dark times.

Me? I am a soldier in the United States Army who has been secretly hoping for orders to deploy once again. Now don't get me wrong. It's nice being surrounded by all the familiar settings of home, wife, children, pets, friends, and places soaked with memories only you know about. I call this environment "life on earth."

Life on earth is great, but maybe that's part of the problem. For a soldier who has become accustomed to being torn away from his or her "earth" and sent to war on what seems to be an entirely different planet, everyday life on an otherwise great earth can sometimes be a little too great to handle—great wife; great kids; great manicured lawn by contracted workers in my great government-provided house and neighborhood; convenient shopping at the military exchange discounted for soldiers; and a great church with all the latest songs, instruments, and electronic gadgets, bringing faith to you through the best subwoofers money can buy. In fact, they don't even mind if I wear sandals and a short-sleeved, floral-patterned shirt at my church, as though I were relaxing on the beach. That might be a good slogan for my church: "Come and relax. We'll wake you up in an hour or so."

That's why I was hoping for orders again. Because away from the greatness of earth on a foreign planet filled with suffering and sorrow, strangely enough, I find I actually put faith, hope, and love into practice the way it was designed to be on a regular and much-needed basis.

When I'm on earth, I hope I get a good parking spot so I don't have to walk all the way from the far side of the church and end up being at the back of the line to get to the coffeepot. On a distant planet (mine being Iraq), I just hoped I got home for the privilege of getting to see that stupid coffeepot again. In fact, I think I'd walk a thousand solar systems just to get to smell the aroma of that coffeepot, which on earth was only one more inconvenience to have to wait for. On earth, things are simply the objects they were created to be, and life can turn into a chore to be accomplished. Deployed to a different planet, they transform into the very hope and inspiration that make earth worth fighting for, surviving for, and coming back to.

Something I've learned away from earth is that fear breeds hope. I don't mean the "I'm afraid I left the garage door open" or "forgot and left the stove on" fears. I mean the "I don't know if I can survive one more day in this environment" fear. Literally. If the nightmares don't overrun your hastily put-together fortifications, then the monotonous daily grind of a soldier's life that keeps exploding into a bad dream will actively seek to tear out all semblance of peace, order, and security from your daily existence. And sustained fear, by necessity, has to kill you or give birth to the hope that life will make sense again once you get back to earth.

The only problem with this hope is that it's like the odds of the "till death do us part" line at the wedding. Sounds wonderful, and the exceptions that get it raise our hopes that we will all get it. But oftentimes, the hope has grown so strong for the earth that's remembered that the earth we actually come home to inevitably pales in comparison.

Earth is still great but not exceptional, green but not verdant, blue but not breathtakingly so. A great earth, but all in all, a disappointment that doesn't measure up until it's back in our memories again, when once more we've left the safety of our earth. It's like the coffeepot at the church. When the last thing you've drunk in close to three days is muddy water near the boiling point, the mental image of that coffeepot is pure silver, dispensing liquid gold. Its percolating steam is a fragrant incense that God shows up to church to smell before tucking the congregation in for their naps. When it's not actually before you as a regular, everyday, tangible object, it becomes a beacon of hope. It has to be left to be missed, but when it is left, it often feels neglected or gets used by too many other hands. But that's just a coffeepot I'm talking about. I think.

As for me, I've got it great on earth. I have a faithful wife with a patriotic heart and the determination to love and support me when I'm on a different planet once again. She becomes my beacon every time—my golden-haired angel, waiting with our cherubim children, witty and smiling, intelligent and perfect. My heaven waiting for me back on earth. But it's not like that with everyone. Some of my fellow soldiers hope with all their hearts to have what I have. I am the bringer of hope. I am the exception that keeps the gamblers throwing the dice. I am proof that not all deployed soldiers become victims of people coming out of the gutters back on earth to drain their precious coffeepots dry of every last drop of hope contained within them.

Thankfully, the process of deploying away from earth is always filled with enough excitement of its own to have to worry about. On each of my deployments, we were inundated with classes, training, and super-important briefings that were mandatory if we were going to be able to get shot at properly.

"You need to write down your escape plan in case you are taken prisoner." The concept being that if I escape, I will, for example, walk toward whatever sun the planet has during the day for two days and then walk with it at my side for the next two days, and so forth. So when a rescue party comes to save my once-captured backside, they can estimate my general location based on my predetermined escape plan.

I never remember what my plan is, and I never seem to factor in the very likely scenario that the first day's travel, at least, will be done at a full-fledged panic run to create as much distance between myself and my former captors as possible. Life is in the details. Hope is in the chance they will figure out where I am despite what I've forgotten to do.

For a month or so, we all, as soldiers in the unit in one form or fashion, initiate our own escape plans from our lives on earth. For several days, we walk face-to-face with family members-and then tactically shift to walking beside them in daily affairs. Then we distance ourselves through various means such as work, meetings, fights, silence, and other nefarious stratagems. Then it finally arrives. We load up, full combat kit on, the ships that will soar through space and take us thousands of miles, years, and planets away from our beloved coffeepots and other such earthly possessions.

This isn't my first mission to another planet, my first combat experience. Heck, the salt-and-pepper flakes in my receding hairline say it's a wonder it's only my second. But missions like these age even the most resilient among us. That's why the military can sell to the government that soldiers need their food to be cheaper and tax-free because of the great sacrifices they make on behalf of a grateful planet. I think they bought off on it with the hope that we might not live as long as civilians and so won't be that much of a financial loss in the long run. It works out that way some of the time. And so a decent retirement benefit package for soldiers is also the dangling carrot that keeps us running.

Everybody knows somebody who knew somebody who actually made it to retirement. This somebody is living the good life on some tropical earthly paradise beach with suntanned bikinied beauties tending to alcoholic beverage orders and hanging on his every word, starry-eyed at a combat veteran hero in their midst, each begging to hear another war story where he single-handedly saved an entire planet by his heroic actions that earned him this or that scar, which they are all too ready to massage for him as though its ache reawakened just with the telling of the tale.

We all become that guy when we are on another planet. We all have stories rehearsed we are going to tell. Those of us who make it back tend to forget those stories when face to face with cameras back on a great earth that still isn't quite exceptional enough to have earned the right to hear the heart and soul of our day-to-day experiences on whatever foreign planet we have just returned from.

Earned. Now that's a word, isn't it? It's a hard word with built-in respect. Not given, not taken ... earned. That's why Soldiers become family after a year away from earth together. They've each earned the right to be good enough to be family. Families often don't earn it; therefore, excess family members who aren't absolutely necessary, to keep the dream of hope alive when off earth, are cast quickly and violently out of the circle of trust and familial relationships. They become "her family," "your family," and, "We're going to see 'them' again?"

The difference is what was earned. I find I love a lot more Soldiers that I personally don't like all that much more than I like relationships I used to love before joining the Service. The difference is what was earned. Like 'em or not, they've earned my respect one long trip after the other. One tear-stained cheek at a time with hand on window as the ship slowly rises away from desperately scared spouses and children clinging to each other. Earned.

Last time I was joined with a group of docs and medics. Combat surgeons in the bloodiest regions of the fiercest fighting in the known universe. Gory stuff. Weird humor too. I remember a surgeon handing me an entire leg he had just amputated from a nineteen-year-old Soldier. I turned to put it in the overused red bio-bag of crushed hope when he pulled it back toward himself.

Thinking he still wanted it, I went to hand it back to him. Maybe he had thought of some way to reattach it. Maybe this kid would have the chance to get a scholarship at a college the military paid for and actually be able to walk across the stage on his own two legs. Hope. It's like an aphrodisiac.

Seeing the hope in my eyes, the doc smiled and said, "No, go ahead and throw it away. I was just pulling your leg."

Bunch of jerks, the lot of them, but I love them. They earned that much from me.

This last time was different. Instead of being in a hospital I was joined with the military police. They are keepers of the worst of the worst, a containment force extraordinaire. Their motto is "Care, Custody, and Control with Dignity and Respect." A tall order when the detainees they hope to apply that motto to are the kingpins of cruelty captured by strategic strikes from the Special Forces, especially to get these ones and twos away from their networks of mass chaos.

These detainees truly are the nightmares that small children fear are coming to snatch them away at night because they were mean to their siblings or refused to eat all of their vegetables at dinner. Those that were captured were placed in the most secure facilities that could be constructed away from earth and set to be watched by the roughest, toughest cops in the universe, whose soft and well smoothed motto seemed strangely at odds with the scarred, life-lined faces with hardened, tired eyes who recited it.

The hot planets are bad. The cold planets are the worst. I have too many twice-healed breaks and injuries that pulse to the surface when they get cold. Nope, I prefer the hot planets, but they are still bad. This particular one didn't cause my leg to ache ... ever. I think it was way too close to its sun, and there was no escaping its strangling, dry heat. It seeped into living quarters, choked out overworked air conditioners, and chapped everything chappable. Sunglasses were a permanent fixture, day or night. The only difference was the clear or dark lenses. You needed them even at night to keep the sand from erasing your pupils one hot gust at a time.

I wasn't sure I even owned a dry T-shirt anymore. Every time I put one on, it was instantly soaked from sweat. It was like a blanket you couldn't take off ... Have I described it enough yet? It was really stinking hot, all the time, everywhere there. And that's where these Soldiers earned their pay.

While walking in the stifling desert heat of Iraq, I would often pretend that I had actually survived to retirement and was just taking a stroll on the beach. As I would pass by other heat sapped officers and support staff that were no doubt day dreaming about their own planet earths, and private beaches, I would picture them in swimming trunks with bright-white smears of suntan lotion on white, pasty, desk-ridden bodies. The illusion never lasted long however, because invariably I would look up and see my fellow Soldiers hunched over with the full weight of their body armor and full kit walking to the transports that would take them to the vaults where nightmares were kept, and the dream of beaches would wash away, leaving only a dry, sandy taste on my chapped lips.

I would really like to tell you that I was a member of the elite Special Forces or that I was the hardcore grunt always silently carrying the brunt of the load in combat. But I can't steal glory I haven't earned. One day I may retell the glory I've seen my brothers and sisters in arms achieve and remember them like they were mine while I'm reclining on my own private retirement beach. Maybe, but right now, that glory is for those who've earned it one long day after another.

My job in the military is a little different than most. I'm a joiner. I get attached to different groups for different missions and end up going native with them for a few years, whether that's on earth or on another planet while deployed to combat. When I lived among the Combat Medics, I became an honorary Combat Medic, and when I was re-stationed to a Military Police Battalion, I earned the privilege of being treated like an honorary MP because I lived, sweated, cried, and hurt as one of them for several years.

Joiners like myself never stay more than two to three years with any particular unit and then are switched around to entirely different groups. That's why I've served with docs and also with MPs. Who knows? Maybe on some future go-around I'll get lucky and join some paper pushers right next to an all-you-can-eat twenty-four-hour-a-day dining facility with a great, big, silver coffee pot that's always full ... Hope. I love it.

Many Joiners I've met seem not to like each other very much but tend to love and to be loved dearly by the various groups they are joined to. There are different kinds of joiners: Cooks, Medics, Supply personnel, Engineers, and others. As for me, if you couldn't tell by my cheery disposition, besides being a Soldier, I'm a chaplain. That's a fancy word for the bringer of hope. I remind Soldiers when the bottom drops out and the worst of the worst has imposed itself upon the best of the best with tragic consequences that God has not forsaken them no matter what it feels like.

This is supposed to be a combat story taking place on a different planet. So you as a reader may be expecting me to tell you about strange alien gods I discovered while on my journeys within the (heretofore) unknown universe or, about the reasoning and logic the world had used to finally discover we are our own gods. Perhaps you might think my exposure to multiple combat experiences had revealed there are no gods and that science is the only hope for understanding the cruelty and ultimate randomness of eternity. Well, first, I would not be a very good bringer of hope if I said that either you or I are the gods we need to have hope in. Second, it's only the ones who have considerably far more faith in the presently unsubstantiated than I do who would claim to be in such an enlightened state as to have achieved inner godhood, or to assert the claim that eternal peace can be found through faith in science. No, I am just a regular sinful person desperately in need of a Savior who just holds stubbornly on to belief in the truth of the Bible even when it's difficult to do so. I believe God still exists. Still loves us. Still doesn't like sin.

Sin. Now there's a word that can get me fired. "Who am I," claim the enlightened ones, "to decide what 'sin' is?" If some choose to do the exact opposite of common-sense living and engage in acts that defy even a cursory knowledge of morality and proper hygiene and I dare to ask the obvious question, "What in Iraq were you thinking?" I become the object of ferocious crusaders for equality and liberalism and the ultimate erasing of anything resembling a standard of any kind. So I tend to engage in fierce combative battles of subtly placed sarcastic wit. I win at least as much as I lose.

Sarcasm is a weapon I've become a master fighter with. I wish sarcasm would win wars, but it doesn't. Screaming, explosions, muzzle flashes, deafening shots, death, anger, shock, and pools of shed blood by young men and women in shredded uniforms now forever silent tend to be the turning points for wars. Sarcasm just helps me survive it.

One particular little piece of the war took place on a planet known as "Operation New Dawn." Some call it Iraq, but what do they know? Planets get named by the ones who conquer them. Operation New Dawn is a nice-sounding name for a place that would more aptly be labeled "Sand Hopelessly in Turmoil." Soldiers have shortened it to New Dawn or OND. But I call it Hope. Hope in the midst of hell fire, long days, loneliness, sadness, fear, anger, and face-slapping letters from home. Hope. It's a great name for a place that lives to breed hope from the worst circumstances imaginable. The coffee pot on earth has never looked as good or contained as perfect a cup of coffee as it has from planet Hope where it is completely out of reach.

THE ARRIVAL

For a Soldier, fourteen-hour plane flights that leave everything familiar thousands of miles behind and cross over oceans, continents, and multiple times zones might just as well be a rocket ship ride to the farthest ends of the galaxy. On my second long voyage through space, with little else to do but think, I couldn't help but remember my first combat mission to the very same strange planet years before. I had heard all the stories of the fierce fighting all over the planet we were headed to—of explosions, direct and indirect fire, IEDs, UXOs, VBIEDs, and a lot of other scary acronyms, but I still had no real idea of what to expect.

The first time over it seemed like it had taken forever to just get ready to go. There were times I wasn't sure it was even going to happen. First, there was all of the training up—"Eight short months to go"—then a trip to the joint regional training center (JRTC) and swimming through a hospital in the middle of Louisiana on the coat tails of hurricane Katrina before we were then allowed to take two weeks leave. After leave came intense training—"Only two short months to go."

PowerPoint presentation briefs were never ending. "We're all winners! Hooah! We beat out four hundred million other sperm just to get to be alive!" These are the only two lines I can remember from endless hours of mind-numbing PowerPoint presentations, and they came from a fellow chaplain giving his suicide awareness class. I guess by that time, I was only paying attention because I thought I might need the help in order to survive another few hours of tedious classes that no one would ever remember.

It was finally time to go. To our final destination? No. To the planet Kuwait, the interstellar gateway to all other planets of interest to the politicians and therefore to the Soldiers of earth. What for? To redo all the classes we had just abandoned precious hours with our families back home to sleep through. But twelve days, multiple smoothies, a painted mural finished by cigarette butts (after my paint brushes were re-acquisitioned by an unknown party), snapped unit photos, and many morale-building visits to the chapel bathroom, and we finally disembarked the Kuwaiti gateway to the stars and came to our military settlement in the Tallil province on planet Iraq. We had made it, but still not entirely. We had to be in tents first, or otherwise the trailers they had for us would only be Motel 6's instead of the Ritz Carlton's they would come to be seen as.

I think back on the year's worth of accomplishments that I had promised myself to complete. They quickly became unrealistically real and so were just as quickly procrastinated off to the last hectic week before redeploying back to the United States. I had been certain I'd be able to lose twenty pounds of fat, gain twenty pounds of sculptured muscle, become a star runner, learn to play the guitar, have a finished masterpiece of an oil painting, write a book, and grow to look several inches taller. I'm a go-getter. I could make it happen.

I just knew the motivation would arrive when I landed on the planet, by which I meant when I got into my permanent living quarters, which turned into meaning when I got into a good routine at work and could start to focus on my personal goals. A definition I eventually had to adjust to mean one week before redeploying and then readjust to mean just as soon as I got back to the States and was able to get away from all of the good DFAC (dining facility) food and stress at work. Ultimately I think I meant … maybe next deployment.

I remember taking great pains to ensure every one of my PT (physical training) uniforms were packed according to the "authorized version" of the packing list: two in my B bag, two in my duffel, several in my tough boxes, one in my A bag, and one in my rucksack. Oh well, so I ran out of shorts by the rucksack. That's all right. I knew I had several in the others, and worst case scenario, I could always purchase some at the PX (Post Exchange) on planet Iraq, which at that time was known as OIF 06-08.

B bag, duffel, and tough boxes remained loaded in connexes and refused to arrive for what seemed like forever. This left me a grand total of one pair of PT shorts and two pairs of white socks. The PX had shorts "extra small." I kid you not. I don't say extra small and mean "large washed one too many times to fit comfortably." I mean actual extra small. Small enough in fact, that it would rapidly become a black thong with a reflective strip down the crack should I try to wrestle a pair on. So one pair of PT shorts and two, wait, one pair of white socks.

Something happened to the other pair of socks. I know I had them packed. I had seen them just a while before, unless the first pair suddenly decided to migrate to a different location for the specific and deceitful purpose of being recounted in my clothing census. Fine! I had one pair of overly used white socks. The good news: there were do-it-yourself washer and dryer laundry trailers just a few feet away from my tent. Problem solved. Wash the precious one pair of white socks nightly until payday when I could buy some more.

From the tent to the laundry, fifty steps. From the washer to the dryer, two steps. Fifty-two steps of pure Bermuda Triangle because in that space only one white sock was allowed passage through our space-time continuum. Honestly. One sock walked with God and then was no more, for God took it.

Mercy, however, was granted by a fellow officer. "Take a pair of my ankle socks."

I had a quandary. My socks had to be worn daily but could not be washed for fear of subjecting the socks to the fifty-two-step Bermuda Triangle "only one sock may pass" policy. I'm afraid he wasn't very eager to get back those overly ripe, sticky banana peels once I finally finished gliding around in them. War is hell ... on socks.

Once we moved from the tents to our more permanent living quarters known as Containerized Housing Units or CHUs, life began to settle into a more predictable routine. Finally getting over jet lag, I launched headfirst into full tourist mode of the local scenery. As it happened, the Ziggurat of Ur loomed proudly and tauntingly in my backyard, defying the passage of time.

This is the (only partially excavated) hometown of Father Abraham, whom I studied about my entire adult life. My children's inheritance was spent paying back the loans paid to the theological schools, who told me wondrous tales of the very place in its (and my mother-in-law's) heyday some four thousand five hundred years ago. I still remember the warning that was given by the tour guide.

"This is only a partially excavated site. You will no doubt find ancient pottery with ancient writing on it and other historically

and theologically significant artifacts just lying around in the sand about you being used and abused by the local insect life."

Smiles and excitement began building inside me to the point where I needed to wipe off saliva that was flowing freely.

"Don't touch the archeological artifacts! Doing so is punishable under the Uniform Code of Military Justice!"

My smile melted to heartbreak and desperate, violent thoughts.

Living the life of a criminal on the run didn't actually seem too terrible of an existence. The kids could entertain the crowds by juggling for our dinners on the lam if necessary. What if an artifact accidentally got scooped up and trapped in my boot? Or my cargo pocket or just happened to fill up three or four of my tough boxes? Surely that would be seen as an unforeseeable accident that I could not be held liable for, right?

Teach me of the wonders of chocolate for years. Show me pictures, describe the taste, create a mental addiction, drive me to Wonka's Chocolate Factory for a year-long night manager's position, and then break the news to me that I'm highly lactose intolerant, and milk chocolate is absolutely out of the question, and see if I don't seize up and die a happy sinner oozing chocolate from every unsealed orifice.

So there I was, stationed right by a major archeological site. Artifacts were just lying around in the sand with the Army base less than a mile away. Most big towns stretch out at least that far. No one said don't pick up artifacts found right outside the dining facility. So I began to look hard among all of the large gravel rocks. They were all shipped here from somewhere, possibly the excavation site.

I kept telling myself, *Pay attention. You could be the one.* I couldn't believe it! My heart skipped a beat! Right there in front of me, I had actually hit the lottery. Amid all the other rocks was one large, cylindrical rock with beveled edges on both ends, obviously man-made. I had done it!

My mind flashed to Southwestern Theological Seminary's archeological museum containing artifacts unearthed from the famous excavation site in mighty Samson's hometown. Among the displays, there was a large, cylindrical rock with Cuneiform writing all around it. It was called a cylinder seal. It was originally created so that after smoothing down clay, the cylinder could be rolled on to it, and several copies of the same letter could be quickly written. It was basically an early copy machine of sorts. It is also a very expensive copy machine on the very top of the "must be purchased" wish list of modern day antiquities collectors.

There at my feet, at least twice the size of Southwestern's puny cylinder, lay my greatest archeological find! I bent over and picked it up. It filled my entire hand. I cradled it so as not to break the ancient rock ... It was heavy.

My inner voice then had a very unpleasant conversation with my frozen body. *Not rock ... metal ... not a cylinder seal. Right on, genius! Apparently you forgot you're over here as a Soldier in a war zone and not as a pastor on an archeological dig.*

My mind then flashed to mind-numbing PowerPoint presentations given several times in the States, in Kuwait, in Iraq ... Why did we have to have these same boring classes over and over and over again? What did they say? *"Do not* pick up any foreign material that does not look like it belongs. The enemy can make improvised explosive devices out of anything."

Not rock ... metal ... not a cylinder seal ... an unexploded piece of ordinance. Slowly and gently I cradled it back to the earth, informed the proper authorities, and watched professionals sweat to remove what I had yanked up barehanded ... gosh I miss that planet.

Mind-numbing PowerPoint presentations filled up the next day. I was riveted! My absolute, undivided, mind-numbed attention given.

"Do not pick up anything that's not yours here. We just recently found unexploded ordinance at the dining facility."

I lowered my head. No eyes were on me. She didn't know the "we" of which she spoke was me.

The one time in my life I think I've actually been happy to have chosen a dud. I love PowerPoint now. I can't get enough of it. I love the endless droning ... I think they're great ... large pizzas floating in a baby-blue sky filled with cuneiform, cylinder clouds ... Where am I? Oh yeah, PowerPoint ... riveting.

With a newfound level of situational awareness, I set about exploring the ancient ruins of the city once known as Ur. The archeological site was situated right outside of the military installation I was stationed on, and its dominant feature was a structure called a ziggurat that looked to me to be identical to a Mayan temple. I remember standing on top of the Ziggurat of Ur in the center of the ancient town.

One of the oldest and most well-preserved ziggurats in the entire world, this particular one had been visited by Abraham himself! What was I doing there? Twitching. My eye was twitching. Why? Because I was surrounded by thousands upon thousands of ancient pieces of pottery, many with the paint still dyed decoratively upon them just as they were thousands of years ago. Pottery and mud-baked bricks with ancient Cuneiform writing on them. All of this and unable to keep any of it! It made my eye twitch.

I walked around the excavated labyrinths of ancient temples, homes, and tombs of both the common and the royal. Each dug out from beneath a mound of dirt. I looked around the surrounding area at hundreds of undisturbed mounds of dirt with unnamed treasures, histories, ghosts, legends, heroes, warriors, families, lovers, and mysteries still greedily buried by the secretive sand; and since I was unauthorized to disturb them, I did the only thing I *was* authorized to do, and that was to disturb myself. And so I twitched.

I climbed down into the earth, into the tombs of ancient Mesopotamian kings and queens, and thanked God for allowing me life and for His presence even there in a room that for centuries had literally been the valley from whence death had cast its shadow. After exiting the tomb, someone called back down into the tomb, thinking I was still there and wanting me to look at something they had found.

I looked over at them and said, "Why do you look for the living among the dead? He is not there."

That was an incredible time in my life. It was kind of like a walk through the Bible. I was able to stand in the remnants of Abraham's home and give Bible studies to Soldiers about how God had called the famous patriarch to leave, well ... from right there. The worst hardship I had to endure during that period of the deployment was the requirement to get dressed in at least PTs in order to walk to the bathroom in the middle of the night.

All I really knew of combat up to that point had come from stories my older brothers had told or what I had seen on television or the movies. The movies, however, tend to be more exciting than reality. Now don't get me wrong. I'm not saying that life doesn't have its adrenaline-saturated points in time. I'm just saying all those points are typically congregated into one two-hour movie, and real life has a tendency to separate those points by long, boring periods of time that most people like to call "every day." And then for those times that do come, it seems they are not up to snuff with true Hollywood-fashion excitement. Take my first encounter with the enemy for example. I was in a rocket attack …

Catchy line, right? Made you want to keep reading, didn't it? At least it was a good hook line to start the salivary glands of the imagination. A line like that breeds all sorts of war story images: pictures of explosions; people running through the night that keeps getting lit up by incoming comets of fiery destruction; random machine gun fire barely muffling gravely, bass voices of salty NCOs barking out orders to fresh recruits who are right in the heart of their first experiences of the "big time" of combat.

My experience differed slightly from that scene. I was standing in the back of a rather long line in the PX in my PT uniform when we heard a muffled boom outside. No one stopped talking. A few Soldiers looked up to see if someone had been working on the roof and had banged it with a hammer of some sort. A second boom, louder this time, rattled the chip bags at my side. Talking turned to silence, and smiles began to widen along with looks at each other as if to say, "Should we be concerned about that?"

A third boom. I could feel the ground shake as though I were inside an empty grain silo that someone had just thrown a large rock at. Silence. Across the PX every head turned as a Soldier's radio, that would normally never have been heard over even mild conversation, squelched a warning that news was coming.

"All Tallil, assume uniform four and move to your bunkers immediately."

Kevlars began flying on all around the room, and a mob of

people surged toward the exit as though the pistol had just gone off, signaling the race had begun.

The race lasted all of fifteen steps as an MP at the entrance bravely halted the stampede. The message was passed quickly down the line that there were no bunkers by the PX and that the safest spot was inside. That news received, I saw my opportunity and took it.

Easing back away from the herd so as not to arouse suspicion, I slowly turned and casually walked back to the now-empty line just in time to hear one of the multitude say, "As long as we're stuck in here, we might as well go back to shopping."

The charge was redirected back into a jockeying for positions in the shopping line, a line in which I was now the first person.

So there I was in my first ever rocket attack. All around me Soldiers were dressed in bullet-proof body armor, Kevlars, M-16s, M-4s, and 9-Mils, all in ready positions. And then there was me standing in my PT shorts and shirt, bravely wielding my upcoming purchase of flowery scented Renuzit air freshener. Life is so exciting!

My one redeeming moment came when a female Soldier behind me, who had gotten nervous after hearing the third boom, said, "I wish there was a chaplain here to pray for us."

I got to turn around in line and smile and say, "You're in luck." And then I got to do what I came to that beautiful planet to do, and that was minister to Soldiers.

That first encounter was followed by other, closer calls. I jumped from planet to planet—Tallil to Mosul to Baghdad—each more shell-shocked than the last. After fifteen months of being mortared, I got to the point where in the middle of the night I wouldn't even leave my room to rush to a bunker during an attack. Instead I would pull my body armor over me like a comforting blankey and drift back into a fitful sleep amidst the reverberating sounds of firefights somewhere in the city just a few hundred feet from my bed.

Life back then in that phase of the war was prolonged boredom continually interrupted by random episodes of sheer terror. The second time over, even though I was walking on the same ground as before, it still felt like an entirely different planet than the one I had served on only a few years prior. In fact, I began to find myself overwhelmed by the sound of silence. I knew I had only been there a short while, but I was on a hostile planet less than a mile from Route Irish that was the flashpoint of hundreds upon hundreds of bombs, attacks, and forever-changed lives. It should be named Patriots' Path because it had been washed with the blood of heroes.

In all the time I was there on my second tour, I did not hear any of the sounds that haunt my dreams and steal in front of my eyes when I'm present but still far away. No prayer calls, no mortars, no crackle of gunfire and wail of sirens. No blaring radio urgently calling for my aid, no purple hearts laid on patriot chest, no smells that evoke instant tears of sorrow.

I was not complaining, nor was I wishing for these things. I was just off guard because of the silence, teetering, unsure of which way to lean—toward belief or toward fear that the lightning was about to strike and the war would suddenly thunder to life at any moment, breeching the eerie silence. Somewhere in the middle was what I attempted with what I believe was a modicum of outwardly achieved success. Inwardly, however, I was waiting and feeling lost without a purpose and at the same time guilty for the sensation.

Silence isn't sadness. It has always been the preceptor of the chaos. Yet minutes have since crept into hours, hours to days,

days to weeks, and the chaos only has shape in the echoes of my dreams, familiar nightmares like welcome friends, comforting in their presence. Nightmares: unseen medals for the privilege of serving next to legends in a time quickly being forgotten by hands rushing to turn the page. Trying to put this strange feeling into words, I wrote a poem to help express my thoughts.

SOUNDS OF SILENCE

Where are the sounds of the guns?
How have the mighty gone silent?
Heroes walk as tourists now
Taking pictures of ghosts from not so long ago.

When the sounds of the guns were the music that filled the night
Blackhawks like predators in the darkness
swooping, screaming—gone
Haunting prayer call piercing silence,
Whistle heralding mortars approach.
Feel the reverberation before sound deafens;
Belated warning prepares for more.

Echoes now, only echoes of a war that defined yesterday,
Wounded today and scarred tomorrow
With glassy-eyed zombies telling tales to nonbelievers
Of the sounds of the guns whose terror now diminished
Is longed for by those whose hearts and souls were shaped
By their sounding, ever sounding, now silenced.
How can they keep rhythm anymore?

How have the mighty gone silent
Now that the streets are filled with dusty silence?
And the guns are gone in all but stories told
By Veterans who were made to age too soon
To wide-eyed Soldiers who seem far too young
Too young, too young to hear the echoes
Of the sounds of the guns.

LET ME SHOW YOU WHAT I LEARNED IN THE ARMY

Soldiers will always be my heroes. When I was a child, my father would come home from work in his Army uniform, and I'd rush to help pull off his boots in the hopes of getting the quarter he had stuffed in the sides of one of them. As I grew, I watched my two older brothers—invincible heroes in my eyes—each don an Army uniform, and I wanted to be just like them.

I remember seeing my eldest brother, Robert, in full gear beside one of the trucks he drove, and I thought he was a green-camouflaged storm trooper from *Star Wars*. My brother Larry wore desert tans (DCUs) and battle dress greens (BDUs) and digitized pattern grays (ACUs), moving up the ranks from E-1 to E-8, a constant true north to set my compass by. I will always look up to my parents and to my big brothers for their valiant service to our great nation, just as I know our children will look up to us for ours.

While growing up, when I saw someone in a military uniform or I met someone who used to be in the Army, to me they instantly became the experts on anything in life. I remember Danny Shanahan. The first time I met Danny, I was fourteen years old in

Fort Mohave, Arizona. My family had just arrived in town, and I found the closest church to our house (First Baptist Church of Ft. Mohave) and started attending. The youth pastor's name was Daryl Shanahan. He took me under his wing and made me feel like I was a part of the group, not just the new guy. Daryl told the youth group one night that his little brother, Danny, was coming home from the United States Army's Basic Training course. I couldn't wait to meet him.

Danny showed up at church the following Sunday in his Class A uniform, and I became his shadow.

"What was basic training like? Have you ever shot anyone? Do you have any tips for me, because I hope to join one day?"

Danny soaked up my hero worship and began to teach me in the Jedi ways of the Army force. Only nineteen, he was still the epitome of cool. He had a car, real-life Army training, and best of all, he let me hang around him.

Most of the crazy things I did as a young man came about as a result of Danny saying, "Let me show you something I learned in the Army."

For instance, one day Danny said, "Stephen, it's time we got six-pack abs. Let me show you something I learned in the Army."

Danny told me Soldiers would throw heavy medicine balls onto each other's tightened stomachs, and the shock to the abs created quick six-packs. Because we didn't have any medicine balls handy, he took out a long tube sock and filled it to the brim with hard Arizona sand (mixed inevitably with some rocks), tied off the end, and said that was just as good. He had me lie down on the ground, and he threw the packed sock at my stomach … It hurt, but I could feel the abs forming.

One or two throws at each other's stomachs inspired him to speed up the process. He went into his father's shed and came out with a ten-foot ladder. He then explained that the greater the distance, the harder the impact, and therefore the faster the growth of the abs. Naturally, because he was the best shot, being Army trained, he would be the first to fire the sock at me. I lay down at the foot of the ladder, closed my eyes, tightened my stomach, and waited for the painful impact. It came … about six inches below my stomach. I couldn't stand properly for hours. Danny assured me that sometimes happened in the Army too.

One day, Danny decided we were taking our sight for granted and needed to have a greater appreciation for those who were blind. He said, "Let me show you something I learned in the Army …" He handed me a blindfold and told me that for an entire day we would both go without sight.

Everywhere we went we had to keep the blindfold on. By that evening at his parent's dinner table, I was bruised and battered from running into things all day long, falling down a flight of stairs, twisting my ankle, and cutting my forehead on a low-hanging tree branch. I was excited the day was coming to a close.

Mrs. Shanahan said, "Stephen, would you mind taking off your blindfold so we can eat dinner?"

I told her, "Ma'am, Danny and I have decided to stay blindfolded all day long to get a better appreciation for those without sight."

Her reply: "Stephen, Danny hasn't had a blindfold on at all today. He's just been walking beside you, watching you walk into things."

Danny told me that sometimes the Army taught hard lessons.

Getting ready for prom, I was again lured into the convincing advice of what my mentor had learned in the Army. He was going to be a chaperone for the dance and felt we both needed to look good for the evening. He decided that would require having a nice tan. I lived in Arizona. I had a built-in tan.

But Danny said, "Let me show you something I learned in the Army ..."

We had five hours until the dance started, so Danny convinced me we needed to speed up the tanning process in order to effectively tan in time. He took out a bottle of "No-Sun Sun Tanning Lotion," and we both stripped down and covered ourselves in it then lay out on lawn chairs. (Danny had no neighbors for miles.) The idea was to combine the tanning effects of the lotion with the natural effects of the sun and thus double the speed in which we tanned.

In order to ensure we tanned evenly on both sides, Danny took out a tape player and put on Air Supply's Greatest Hits. After every song, we were supposed to flip over. When the tape was done, we would be too.

I awoke two hours later to the sound of Danny snoring. I looked over at him and screamed.

He awoke with a start, saw me, and returned the scream. "Stephen! You're orange! And blistered!"

We had fallen asleep during the very first song and then baked in the Mohave Desert for two hours. The lotion turned our skin a bright orange, and the sun blistered us everywhere. My date danced with a lot of other people that night.

I have now completed basic training twice: once as an enlisted Soldier and once as an officer. I have also spent over fifteen years in the Army since graduating basic training and have been deployed to combat twice. Even with all of that experience, I still have not learned a third of the things Danny Shanahan convinced me he had learned in the time he spent in initial Army training, but Danny remains one of my heroes, because like my big brothers and like my father, he served in the Army that I love so much.

I met someone recently who reminded me that fathers can look up to sons just as much as sons can look up to their fathers. I was sitting on a wooden bench in front of fully up-armored tactical space vehicles and huddled around a small, well-worn chess set with several chess pieces that had been reglued together. As the sun was beginning to set on Camp Cropper, Planet Hope, I asked the gentleman sitting across the board from me a question. "How long have you been in the military, Sergeant Smith?"

Sergeant Smith looked about sixty-five years old but was just in his mid fifties. The effect was enhanced by the fact that he had just come off of a mission, and his deep-seated facial creases were lined with dark, dried dirt.

"Fifteen years now, Sir. I was going to get out, but my son changed my mind."

"Your son changed your mind?"

"Yes, Sir. I had done my time, and my son convinced me to reenlist. I wasn't going to, but then he got killed while fighting in Kirkuk, and I signed back on in honor of his service. He died fighting two years ago today."

I saw a wet streak of grime run down his face without embarrassment. I asked if I could pray for him and his family on this, the anniversary of his son's sacrifice. Sixteen hats flew off dirty, bowed heads, and I prayed my heart out. When I finished I reached my finger over to my king and slowly set it on its side ... Soldiers will always be my heroes.

I'm sure Green Beans exist somewhere on earth, but I've only ever seen them on military FOBs (Forward Operating Bases) off world. It's funny. Off planet in the barren, tan desert I drank at Green Beans. On good old green terra firma, I drink at a place called *Star*bucks. Go figure. I am addicted to spice chai lattes from Green Beans. They taste like melted pumpkin pie. I was impatiently waiting for my fix to be fixed when Sergeant Smith walked in to get his daily dose of liquid sunshine. As soon as he saw me, he broke into a big smile and said he had been looking for me.

Apparently, after I had finished our game of chess and prayed for him, his family, and his unit's protection, Sergeant Smith's group was called out on a mission. Someone had been spotted digging a hole near the camp. As a side note, if you are a treasure hunter and decide to go digging for some of the oldest treasures in the galaxy, I would recommend doing it somewhere far away from the watchful eyes of a US Military installation, as it will quickly summon a large group of well-armed Soldiers hopped up on caffeine and a little disgruntled at having been called away from their spice chai lattes. Anyway, when they reached the location, no one was in sight, and they proceeded to do a dismounted reconnaissance of the area. Just then, from some unseen location, our aforementioned treasure hunter detonated his buried IED.

A few hours later, Sergeant Smith's wife received a phone call on the anniversary of her son's death. It was from her husband telling her that he loved her. Due to some miscalculation, or hasty plant, (or perhaps Divine intervention), not a single Soldier or vehicle was harmed by the detonation. The spice chai latte sat forgotten on the counter as Specialist Nelson, Captain Murragurah, Sergeant Smith, and I huddled in a circle in the middle of Green Beans on an isolated little planet called Hope and thanked God for a Father's protection.

Laughter is good medicine. Sometimes when things are so incredibly wrong, it is a survival skill to see the ironic and humorous side of life and allow your inner audience to applaud and laugh. In fact, there are times it's difficult to hear the idiocy of the one in front of me because he is being drowned out by the roar of laughter in my head. Mastering a deadpan facial expression is also a survival skill when the object of irony outranks me, as he or she often does.

The problem with developing such a great skill set is that it longs for expression and to be shared with others. Like watching the movie *Anger Management*. If Adam Sandler had heard us laughing at the ridiculous way he was being treated by everyone around him, he might have had a much more pleasant experience. This is where cartooning came into my life.

Throughout history there have been cartoonists. In fact, I bet when the woman caught in adultery was brought to Jesus by the hypocritical crowd and the Bible says Jesus bent down and began to draw in the sand with His finger, He probably drew a cartoon of a kettle calling the pot black. Some situations are so obviously ridiculous that it can only make those involved feel better when someone points out the punch line.

I remember when I went through basic training in Fort Jackson, South Carolina, in 1996. Sergeant First Class Johnson, a six-foot giant of a man, pressed the brim of his Drill Sergeant's hat against my forehead and screamed at the top of his lungs, "Do I look stupid to you, Private?"

That was the first time I learned that mastering the deadpan expression would be a very valuable survival skill. One unrepressed chuckle caused me hours of misery and pain.

By the end of basic training, I had won the award for the highest physical fitness, not because I was more motivated, but because by that time I had had more experience than any other Soldier at doing pushups. I also had a sketchpad full of cartoons.

One of the things Soldiers do in basic training as a type of culminating event for all of their newly learned ninja warrior skills is to go to the field and camp out for a few days. Our company, Bravo 161 "Killer Maddogs," was in the process of moving to a new building when our camping trip was scheduled.

We arrived in the woods, and Sergeant First Class Johnson pointed at me and yelled "Pri!"—"Private" was always too exhausting to say, I suppose—"Pri! Get over here!"

I walked over and was told to take off all of my gear. I naturally assumed I was due for some more pushups for something I had said or done.

After stripping off my Load Bearing Equipment (LBE) and Kevlar, I awaited the order to "beat my face," which meant do pushups until the Drill Sergeant remembered I was there.

Instead he said, "Pri! I said take off all your gear. Get that top off."

So I removed my BDU top, leaving just my brown T-shirt.

"Get your entrenching tool and dig a hasty fighting position right there." He pointed at a thick tangle of poison oak.

"Drill Sergeant, that's poison—"

"I didn't tell you to talk! Do I look stupid to you, Pri?" He eyed every flicker of my eyelids to make sure I had zero response.

I was a master of the deadpan now. My inner audience went wild. I dug for less than five minutes when he told me to stop.

"Take off your shirt, Pri!"

I stared silently.

"I will stick my boot through the center of your chest if you do not execute the order, Pri!"

I took my shirt off.

"Get into your fighting position, Pri!"

I looked down at all of the poison oak still bristling out of the scratch in the hard ground I had managed to make. "Drill Sergeant ..."

"Now, Pri!"

I lay down directly on top of several branches of poison oak and instantly began itching.

"Roll over, Pri!"

I rolled over.

"Get up, Pri. Let's get you to the medical clinic. Don't you know that's poison oak? I swear, they make Privates dumber every cycle."

I put my shirt back on and silently went to the medical clinic to receive copious amounts of calamine lotion. Then instead of driving me back to the field, the Drill Sergeant veered off to the new building the company was moving into. I knew this was where he would finally kill me. Inside the new company office there was a chair, paint, paintbrushes, a six-pack of Cokes, and a stack of chocolate candy bars.

"The only way you could be removed from the field was for

medical reasons, Pri. Do you think you could paint a mural of all the Bravo Company Drill Sergeants on our new office wall?"

I was left by myself for three blessed days to paint and scratch, interrupted only occasionally by Drill Sergeant Johnson bringing me more contraband sodas and candy. Seeing the funny in that experience and many others still makes it a joy instead of a trauma to remember. It also gives me hope that there will be a punch line somewhere in the future for whatever current trauma I am trying to survive.

I found a lot of personal need for, and inspiration for, cartoons during basic and later in Korea. I spent a lot of time drawing, finding hope in the punch lines of events that would have otherwise overwhelmed me with anger and bitterness. For example, I remember in basic training, Jennifer called to tell me she had gotten pregnant during our honeymoon. I assured her I would be home after Advanced Individual Training (the specialized skill training that follows every Soldiers basic training), and then we would spend the rest of our lives together. I came home after AIT to tell her that in two weeks I was being shipped to a strange planet called Korea for an entire year without her.

I stepped off the plane in Korea and sunk to my knees in snow. I knew then God either shared my sense of humor, or He hated me. I wasn't driven to a barracks. I was instead driven directly to the field where my new company, the 302nd Forward Support Battalion, was living in tents for an entire month for an exercise called "War Steed."

I found my designated tent only to discover the chaplain I was supposed to be assisting was a very grumpy female wrapped up in a sleeping bag on a cot who introduced herself by saying, "It's about time, Specialist. Put this heater together!"

There was a cardboard box in the middle of the tent, and

inside was a World War II–style stovepipe heater. It looked like a barrel cut in half with several sections of pipe to fit together for a chimney. I worked all night trying to read the directions by a red lens flashlight to the melodious sounds of the chaplain scorning whatever training I neglected to get in Basic that made me inept at putting together a simple heater.

By 0500 the next morning, it was finally assembled and actually started to warm the tent. The chaplain rolled out of her sleeping bag to warm her hands against its side.

I sat on the edge of my cot to do the same, and she said, "What are you doing? It's stand to. Get outside with your weapon and guard the perimeter."

My inner audience applauded and laughed raucously. I didn't.

Later that night I discovered I should have read the maintenance section of the directions because it would have told me the stove needed to be cleaned of soot daily. I had just wrapped up in my sleeping bag when all of the soot that had collected in the stovepipes back drafted into the tent, turning the entire living space into a black cloud like the Ark of the Covenant had just been opened in an Indiana Jones movie.

Two white eyes glared at me through the darkness. "I hate you" was all she said before she loaded up the HMMWV (which is the Army talk for Humvee) and headed back to the base, leaving me to finish the month-long field problem on my own.

The S-1 section took oversight control of me while the chaplain was gone and moved me into a community tent with forty other Soldiers. The Staff Sergeant in charge of the section seemed to be bitter at life in general and loved the opportunity to make everyone around him view life just as sourly. He was apparently disgruntled at being unable to give me tasks throughout the day, as I was an entirely different, although one-man, section of my own.

In order to fix this problem, he put me on permanent fireguard for the tent, which involved sitting up at night in two-hour shifts and watching the heater so that it didn't catch any sleeping Soldier on fire. In the morning, it was my job to scrub out the soot so it didn't back draft again.

I had just finished my second shift at 0200 in the morning and needed to go to the latrine. The port-a-johns were roughly a half-mile walk through the snow, and the policy was you had to wear all of your combat gear anytime you left the tent. So I put on my jacket, gloves, LBE, Kevlar, and M-16 and tromped through the frozen night to find a latrine. Once inside the narrow rectangle, the wrestling match was on to take off all that gear to get to the necessary equipment required to pee.

In the darkness I heard plop … plop. I froze in the middle of taking off my jacket, turned on my flashlight, and peered fearfully into the blue, murky water in the toilet. There in a steaming pond of sewage were my sinking gloves. I still had over three weeks left in the snow. I needed those gloves. I had a decision to make. Rolling up my sleeves, I reached in and pulled out the dripping nastiness.

Scrubbing them in the snow took away the blue sani-water color, but the smell was horrible. I carried them back to the tent with two fingers. As I entered the tent, the first cot I came to belonged to the S-1 Staff Sergeant. I noticed he had an identical pair of black gloves on the end of his cot to warm by the fire he had doomed me to be the "watcher of." I had a decision to make.

The next morning the Staff Sergeant yelled at me, "Specialist Dicks! Get this stove cleaned! How many times do I have to tell you?"

That was the first time he had ever had to tell me, but I let it go as I saw his face suddenly contort, as he brought his gloved hand to his nose and nearly choked. "What in the—" was all I heard him yell as I took my roasty toasty gloved hands outside to clean the stovepipes. My inner audience cheered.

The same Staff Sergeant put me on a night-shift detail to string concertina wire around the entire perimeter of our field post. For those that don't know, concertina wire is like barbed wire on steroids. Instead of twisted barbs, it has rows on rows of razor blades. It takes special gloves just to handle the stuff; but uniforms, arms, legs, and every other nongloved area of all your Lever 2000 parts are still in constant danger.

This detail began around midnight, and by 0130, it had begun to sleet and pour down freezing rain. The sloped Korean hillside turned into a mix of snow and mud, and the final hill to carry the concertina wire up was rapidly becoming an impossible mission. The six of us on the detail kept trying to hoist the roll of wire and scramble up the muddy slope only to slide back down again, drenched, muddy, and more cut up than the previous attempt.

That's when I got the brilliant idea of making a human ladder. I told the lowest ranking Private to lie down in the mud. The next Soldier climbed up his body and lay down, resting his boots on the Private's shoulders. When everyone was in place, I hoisted the mound of wire on to one arm and began climbing up the human ladder I had created. It was working perfectly until about halfway up I heard someone yelling over the roar of rain. I looked down to see a soaked First Lieutenant.

"Is there a Specialist Dicks up there?"

I called back down, "Yes, Sir. I'm Specialist Dicks."

He called back up, "You just had a daughter! Congratulations. Now get back to work."

Lightning flashed, and thunder struck on cue. I was a dad! I heard a peal of shouts and yells. I thought at first my ladder crew was cheering for me, until I realized they were cussing as I had let the circle of razor wire roll out of my hands in a straight line down the tops of every one of them. My inner audience was wheezing.

My next duty station to Fort Bliss, Texas, was filled with enough material to fill up a thousand sketchbooks. Therefore, I began drawing cartoons for the military newspaper *The Fort Bliss Monitor*. I called the cartoon "Another Monday" because everything ironic seemed to make life feel like the beginning of another long week.

The cartoon was about me and all of the ridiculous situations I found myself in as a Soldier. Apparently, other Soldiers related to them as well, and the cartoons were a hit. Thankfully, officers at the General level tended to have similar senses of humor to the everyday Soldier, and so I was finally given some latitude for my sarcasm.

Each post I went to afterward, I would draw for them, even after accepting a commission as a chaplain. *The Fort Bliss Monitor, The Fort Bragg Paraglide, The Ingleside Index, The Fort Leavenworth Lamp, The Dugway Dispatch,* and *The Fort Hood Sentinel* all became weekly printers of my life in cartoons. Apparently I had a gift for helping others find the punch line in painful circumstances and in so doing offered them a welcome smile and hope for a happier tomorrow.

I took my pencil and paints with me to the strange planet of Iraq, and they became a lifeline of sanity for me and many others. Throughout both deployments, seeing the mundane, tragic, ridiculous, and routine circumstances of life through a humorous lens was like spoonfuls of medicine to ailing souls. To see sparks reignite in tired eyes and grins twist on heavy smiles refilled my energy as much as it did theirs.

In 2007, in Baghdad, I would draw cartoons for wounded children in the hospital and then give them crayons to color them in. I would draw pictures of Iraqi patients taking the medicine the doctors had prescribed to them so they could understand the instructions until an interpreter could come over. Pictures make up a universal language that crosses every barrier. I could speak fluent cartoon, and the patients enjoyed listening. To hear their laughter in the midst of horrible injuries is the biggest blessing I can ever hope to receive.

So I put my pencils, pens, paints, and brushes to work on a regular basis to draw hope for Soldiers, to bring color to a tan landscape and laughter to a planet that seldom hears it. I painted twelve-foot murals on the top of the hospital emergency room while standing on my tiptoes on the top rung of a ten-foot ladder. I put my First Sergeant on permanent weapons guard by painting his life-sized portrait with a message that told Soldiers to clear their weapons before entering the building. I painted murals of the companies I served with in Kuwait, in Tallil, in the "Green Zone" of Baghdad, in Mosul, in Camp Cropper, and in Al Asad, Iraq. Every stroke of the brush brought smiles, and every sketch brought hope. I drew pictures of our fallen heroes as memorials to them in Iraq and in the United States. I drew parodies of events and seemingly insane senior leaders that got passed around like secret gossip by laughing Soldiers.

Soldiers began to come to me and give me ideas for new cartoons. The ideas sprang from events that happened in their own lives, events that at the beginning of the deployment would have weighed heavily on their shoulders and threatened to tear them down. Now, somehow they had been empowered to view life through my eyes, the eyes of laughter and irony, sarcasm and humor. I found that I was drawing hope ... one picture at a time.

THE STORYTELLER

Combat Veterans are a unique breed of people. They also tend to be expert storytellers. You can always tell a true combat Veteran by the entourage he has around him as he nonchalantly weaves his spell of death, destruction, narrow escapes, hair-raising chases, fire fights, and quaint love for all things common back on earth.

One particular combat Veteran, Sergeant First Class Eddy Ford, always has me in his circle of rapt attention-givers when he starts talking. He has been on every foreign planet the corps has had a mission to for the past fifteen years. The stuff most of the new recruits grew up learning about in junior high and high school, he participated in.

If the mood catches him just right, he will tell you he was the main cause of starting or finishing missions in this or that decisive battle. It's a true art, telling a great story. Most people try imitating the greats. I know I do. But there's something about timing, inflection, and having actually done remarkable things under impossible circumstances that adds a level of intensity and validity to a truly great story. Sergeant First Class Ford tells truly great stories every time he speaks.

Most people answer a question with a simple yes or no,

especially when speaking to an officer who has a senior rank and a superior opinion of themselves. Not Sergeant First Class Ford. His answers typically sound something like this: "Well, Sir, that's a great request. It reminds me of the time I got my left ball shot off during the initial invasion in '03. No one thought we were coming out alive. Honestly, I didn't think I would come out alive for sure. Then a junior officer who was convinced he knew the right way to engage the enemy because he had graduated Suma Cumae So-the-F-What from the Army War College stood up and made a similar request to the one you just made."

Sergeant First Class Ford would shake his head and continue. "Now we all knew it was a stupid request, as you can imagine, Sir. You're a smart person. But because he outranked me, and I always respect my superior officers, I jumped up from cover in the midst of a firefight. I dropped everything else I was doing to protect the post and my fellow Soldiers so that I could complete the ridiculous task he had just given me. Well, no sooner had I gotten to the officer's position, when a sniper shot my left ball clean off. His second round blew the officer's head right off his shoulders. Blew it up like a watermelon.

"Now I like you, Sir. And I like my one remaining nut. Because I like you, I feel the need to protect you. I promised myself if I ever made it off that planet alive, I would never endanger my remaining testicle or get my favorite officer's head shot off ever again. So please don't ask me to drop the important things I'm doing right now that are helping to protect the lives of fellow Soldiers just to watch you get killed, Sir. I can't in good conscience do it."

And then he would walk away from a bewildered officer, smiling all the way.

Later he confided in me conspiratorially that he never actually got his testicle shot off. It was nothing that dramatic. Instead he said it was more like the time when he had contracted leishmaniasis disease from completely unsanitary living conditions while in extended combat operations on some planet or other during the historically bloody Surge Operations of '07. "But," he would say, "that's a different story."

Sergeant First Class Ford always likes to prep the battlefield for another great story at some point in the future.

The one time in his military career that he actually "dropped the ball," Sergeant First Class Ford would say, he did so literally. "That was back in '06. The ball actually just kind of rotted away." He told me. "It's all right, though. They replaced my ball with a plastic one. They brought me out this menu, and I got to order a new one like I was at dinner. Did I want the Brad Pitt model or the Mel Gibson special? I went with the Schwarzenegger. Every day they had docs and nurses from this local hospital come in and check out my junk.

"Now I'm not in a military hospital. I'm on a foreign planet with people I can't understand at all. Once a day a nurse would come in and, in broken English, ask me how I'm feeling then hike up my gown to examine my new plastic feature. One day a new nurse came in and asked me how I was doing, and so I just hiked up my gown and pulled out my junk to show her. She screamed and ran out. I thought I must have something seriously wrong for a reaction like that. About five minutes later my normal doctor came in to tell me I had just flashed the cleaning lady with my Schwarzenegger. I never saw her again. And that's why you don't get seen in foreign hospitals."

This wasn't the first time I'd had the pleasure of meeting Sergeant First Class Ford. My previous combat tour with the mighty Airborne 28th CSH docs and medics put me right in the heart of the greatest pain, suffering, carnage, and heroism that

I have ever seen in my life or even read about in science fiction stories! Every day we got Soldiers brought to us to fix. In the course of my mission as the bringer of hope, I would listen to their stories. I am not a master storyteller and fear I could not do them justice if I tried to retell those stories, but the very memory of some of their tales still bring tears to my eyes.

I remember a female flight medic sitting in the waiting area of the ER. She had just flown in a load of two KIAs (Killed In Action) and three wounded. She looked so dazed in the hallway, slowly rocking back and forth like she was a mother rocking her child to sleep. Her eyes were wide and glazed, and her lips were working furiously but not making a sound, like she was having a conversation in her head. I bent down in front of her, and it took a few seconds for her to realize I was even there. When her eyes focused and she saw my joiner symbol, a cross on the upper-right chest of my uniform, she burst into tears and threw her arms around me like a drowning person clinging to a floatation device.

She told me she was engaged to a Special Forces Soldier. They were planning on taking R &R together in two weeks to get married. She got the call to pick up a group of wounded who were in a firefight in the city. When she arrived there were already two KIAs, one of whom was her fiancé. She helped load his body onto the Black Hawk and had to ignore it the entire trip so she could focus on frantically trying to save the lives of the other critically wounded Soldiers on his team. It wasn't until just then that she had been able to stop and let the full weight of what had just happened to all of her hopes and dreams envelop and crush the life out of her.

"It's funny," she said. "Yesterday I was so worried about what my award was going to be and who I was mad at and what so and so thought about me. Now it's all so unimportant, like it never was important."

Soldiers always help me get my priorities straight.

One day a group of tired, dirty, blood-soaked troops rushed into the hospital carrying two critically injured people in their arms. One was their fellow brother, and one was the nightmare that had shot him. Both were injured to the point that death would come soon if not for heroic and miraculous actions on the part of the overworked surgeons, medics, and staff. They brought both of them into the ER and lay them on beds side by side with only a thin hanging sheet between to separate them. This was normally never done, enemy and friend side by side, but there were so many bad days that week, every available spot was taken, and time was of the essence.

Two groups working on identical injuries side by side in full view of the long hallway lined with praying Soldiers. Dirty weapons attached to every opening on blood soaked body armor. Blackened faces streaked clean by sweat and tears. None of them would be moved an inch to the waiting area; all wanted to see the outcome. On the right, efforts slowed and stopped. A watch was checked and the sheet lifted over the head of an American patriot.

An eruption like multiple mortar rounds exploding at once rippled down the hallway as Soldiers realized what had happened and lashed out with yells, screams, punching walls, sliding down into crouched positions on the ground to give into weeping, and lots of unashamed hugging by the fiercest fighters in the universe.

Off on the left, the team continued feverously working to save the life of the one who just ripped life away from their brother. As they were cutting away his clothes, I heard a string of curses.

I overheard the doc say, "He's got a colostomy bag already, and it's one of ours. That means we've already saved this one before and put him back on the streets."

I could read it on their faces. All they had to do was stop. Give shallower compressions, withhold that extra bag of blood, turn off this or that switch for just a second or two. All they had to do was become him, and they would have revenge. Instead they kept working.

Seeing that he would need more blood than they had on stock, a call was put out over the loudspeaker for any Soldier who had an A Positive blood type. It was needed for a donation to save a life. I kid you not, but some of those crushed Soldiers in the hallway in the heart of their grief struggled to their feet, took off their weapons and body armor, rolled up their sweat-soaked sleeves, and gave their own life blood to save the enemy. These are the heroes I keep serving for. I don't care what the media says about our troops. I have seen them at their best fighting the galaxy's worst. There are none like them, and they give me hope.

It was while training up to come back to that particular piece of hell in the universe that I first saw Sergeant First Class Ford sitting by himself smoking a giant cigar. Part of my job as a joiner (chaplain) is to pick up on when someone might need a listening ear or a friend for a while, so I walked over and sat down beside him looking up at all the stars, wondering which one we'd be fighting and dying on in the future, and I started listening to one of his stories for the first time. I've been hooked ever since.

In that particular story, he talked about the reason he always wears a black bracelet on his arm. On it is inscribed the name of one of his Soldiers he lost on a hot planet in the province of Mosul during an attack. He said he was partial to joiners because when they got his Soldier to the CSH, the joiner there took great pains to ensure he and his men were able to see the body of their fallen brother and honor him in their own ways and just get the privilege of saying good-bye.

After a few questions about dates, times, and locations, I asked, "Did the chaplain look anything like me?"

He paused, took a good look at me, and said, "You were the chaplain!"

Since then it seems like he feels the need to protect me and include me in his stories as one of his close friends. I think, sometimes, I'm the officer whose head he's trying to save along with his left nut.

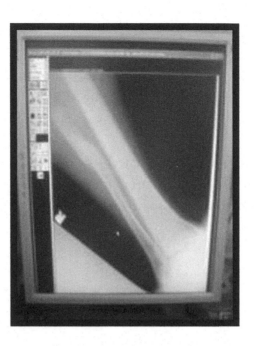

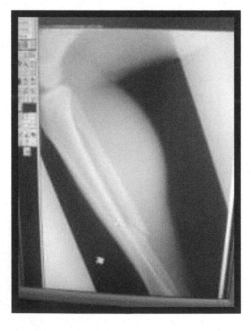

A BREAK IN SERVICE

I run with a limp. I suppose it's not a very noticeable limp to anyone but me, but I know it's there because it hurts. I've run with a limp for seventeen years now, mostly because that's how long my leg has been broken.

In 1998, I was an E-4, a Specialist in the United States Army serving as a Chaplain Assistant in Ft. Bliss, Texas. My wife, Jennifer, and I knew God had been calling us to the chaplaincy, but there were so many unknowns that it was pretty scary. Mainly, how would we eat if I got out of the Army in order to go back to college? Many Soldiers joined the Army with the Montgomery GI Bill that would pay for their school. I had come in with a bachelor's degree and almost sixty thousand dollars worth of college loans. I opted for the College Loan Repayment Program, which successfully erased that debt for me but left any future college up to my own wallet.

There were also multiple hoops to be jumped through, as is the case with anything worthwhile. I needed to be licensed and ordained by my church as an official minister of the Gospel (about a six-month process for my denomination), then apply for acceptance at an accredited seminary (a mountain of essays using big, scholarly words), then apply through the Army for acceptance into the Chaplain Candidate program (a second mountain of essays only utilizing Army acronyms), and finally I had to apply for acceptance in the Chaplain Candidate program through the North American Mission Board (a third mountain of essays using copious amounts of church lingo). The whole process would take just over a year once started, and if I was successful, I would have earned my way out of a paying job, house, and medical benefits. Having two daughters to care for, it was tough to see the upside.

I have very seldom been accused of having common sense. Byron Barnes, my pastor growing up, used to tell me, "Son, I buy you books and buy you books, and you eat the pages."

That being the case, we dove headfirst into the mountain of reasons others said "would never happen," and if I may be allowed a little chaplain moment here, by faith told the mountain to get out of the way ... and it did (one shovel full of hard work at a time).

By June of 1999, I had been accepted as a student to Southwestern Baptist Theological Seminary in Ft. Worth, Texas. Brother Ron Fox from Valley View Baptist Church had presented my family to the church and in a ceremony conferred on me a certificate of licensure and a certificate of ordination as a "Minister of the Gospel of Jesus Christ." The North American Mission Board had met and voted to accept me as a candidate for military chaplaincy, and the United States Army Board had met and called to say I was officially accepted into the Chaplain Candidate program. The last thing to do was to take off my Specialist rank and pin on Second Lieutenant bars.

My older brother, Larry, was an E-6 Staff Sergeant on Ft. Bliss at this time, and even though he wasn't in my unit—he was with the Patriot Missile people—he took great pleasure in seeing me at random times on the post and hazing me until he got bored.

He would call, "Hey, Specialist! Get over here! High speed."

I knew at that point it would be no good running. After all, he of all people knew where I lived.

"Did you shave today, Soldier?"

"Yes La—. Yes, Sergeant."

"Were you just about to refer to me with some kind of familiar title? I tell you what, Specialist, from now on, you can call me by my first name."

"Larry, I—"

"My first name is Sergeant! Get down and do some flutter kicks. Did you shave today, Specialist?"

"Yes, Sergeant," I would say while lying on my back on the concrete, kicking my legs up and down.

"Next time you need to stand closer to the razor."

When I would finally be given the order to "recover," he would look in disgust at my now obviously wrinkled uniform. "Did you iron your uniform today, Soldier?"

"Yes, Sergeant."

"Was the iron on?"

And so on and so forth for the two years we served together at Fort Bliss. He came to my promotion ceremony to officially promote me to an officer alongside Jennifer, a promotion that finally allowed me to outrank him.

In a time-honored tradition, I had chosen him to be the first enlisted Soldier to salute me and to receive as a reward a silver dollar.

As he saluted me in front of several full-bird Colonels, my wife and daughters, our mother and older brother, Robert, he whispered under his breath, "You better watch closely because this is the last time I will ever do this, and if you *ever* try to do to me what I have done to you, I will kill you because I still outrank you in the family."

I don't think he was speaking metaphorically, so I have never challenged that statement, and probably never will.

Despite having Second Lieutenant rank, I was officially out of the active duty Army with no pay, no benefits, no house, and no job. I could apply for thirty to seventy days' active duty at a time in between college semesters, and during that time would have all the benefits of the Army, but other than that I needed a job quickly. I began applying for jobs as a youth pastor at different churches and was finally accepted at a church about two hours away from the seminary in Dawson, Texas. We wouldn't be making very much money, but it had a two-bedroom apartment attached to the youth building. It used to be the high school AG barn, and we could live in it rent-free. Our house was appropriately named, "The Youth Barn."

Each morning I would wake up at around 4:00 a.m., drive the two hours to seminary, take four classes, and then drive home to get ready for youth group activities. Making less than minimum wage, I did odd jobs for people in the church to afford groceries and gas. We were very hungry. To this day if you walk in my house, something will be cooking. If you leave without eating, Jennifer will get her feelings hurt. We went so long with so little, that every chance we get we try to give at least something to struggling families.

In November of 2000, we took one of our high school youth group members (whom we had just received legal custody of) with us to Jennifer's grandmother's house for Thanksgiving. We had been roughhousing throughout the day—he trying to prove why he was the best wide receiver on the football team, and I was trying to prove I wasn't old. I had gone into the woods with my brother-in-law Adam to gather firewood to sell when Kendrick, the youth member, saw my back turned and a perfect opportunity for an unobstructed tackle. He didn't see that I was standing with my right foot in a hole.

He tackled me and twisted so I would land semi-painfully, and that's just what happened right after the loud *crack*! My foot had remained in the hole during the entire tackle and twist. I pulled it out and thought in a kind of semi-detached manner that I must have lost my foot somewhere. Actually it had come out of socket and completely rotated to the rear, so I was looking at my heel instead of toes.

I looked at Adam and said, "When the shock wears off, I bet this is really going to hurt." It's almost like I'm a prophet or something because it really did hurt when the shock wore off! Incredible.

Adam helped load me into his pickup truck, and we did ninety-eight mph to the local hospital. When we got there, being a former Airborne Soldier with the 82nd, Adam decided he needed to do a fireman's carry to get me into the hospital. I told him I was fine and to go get a wheelchair, but he wasn't hearing anything I was saying. Combat maneuvers were in full swing. As my leg was beginning to throb and I was starting to get nauseated, I capitulated to his heroic efforts.

He threw me over his shoulder, and outweighing him by several pounds, we looked like a lopsided T lumbering up to the automatic sliding doors of the ER. T's, by the way, don't fit well into narrow doorways, as we discovered when my head slammed into one door frame, and my broken right leg slammed into the other.

"My bad, brother." He grunted, turned me lengthwise, and shuffled me into the ER a little more dazed than before.

The female doctor on duty that night weighed all of ninety pounds. I sat up on the bed as she began cutting off my shoe.

She looked at me and said, "We may have to amputate."

I smiled. "May means other options get considered first, right?"

She nodded. "I'll try to set it first and see what kind of nerve damage was done. Are you ready?"

"Absolutely." Well, actually I said, "Ab—holy cow!" as she pulled my inverted foot straight toward her and tried to spin it around.

The first two yanks were unsuccessful, and I was laughing really loud to keep from crying.

"Doc," I said, "you're just pulling my leg, aren't you?"

Adam was laughing, the doctor was laughing, and I was laughing. They were laughing, because apparently they mistook my laughter for having a good time.

She was prepping for another pull, when I asked, "Can I get some pain medication, please?"

"I'm sorry, Sir. We can't give you any more than the nurse gave you when you first came in."

"Ma'am, you are the only person I've seen since we made it through the front door."

I saw her face noticeably blanch as she looked for a medical chart. "No one gave you anything?"

"No, ma'am, we walked in, and you began playing the tuba with my leg."

"Sir, I am so sorry. When I heard you laughing and telling jokes, I thought you were heavily medicated!"

I got all the medication I wanted after that.

It turns out the muscles in my leg had contracted so tightly that she wasn't strong enough to rotate it back in place. To fix this problem, she got a hulk of a man out of the X-ray department, who told me he had never set a bone in his life, "but it seems pretty straightforward." It only took him one turn, and I saw my toes again as my ankle slipped back into socket.

My ankle and my right fibula were both broken. They did surgery multiple times to put screws in my ankle and six months later to take them out again. They said the fibula being a non–load-bearing bone would heal on its own. I traded Greek tutoring lessons to a physical therapist in my seminary to reteach me how to walk. I slowly transitioned from being bedpan, bedridden to crutches, to a cane, to a limp.

Each morning at 4:00 a.m., Jennifer would get up, load me and our two daughters into the car, and drive me the two hours to seminary. As she was pregnant once again with our third daughter, I would steer with my left hand while she drove, throwing up into a bag with morning sickness ... Good memories, good times.

When we discovered Jennifer was pregnant, I applied for a youth pastor position at a church that could feed us and was accepted at the First Baptist Church of Holliday, Texas. Tina was born in Wichita Falls right outside of Holliday, and we served at the church there for just over a year before moving to First Baptist Church of Ingleside, Texas, right outside of Corpus Christi. My son Stephen was born in Corpus Christi, and I finally graduated my four-year degree in just over five.

May 17th 2005, in Fort Bragg, North Carolina, Jennifer and the then Chief of Chaplains, Major General David Hicks, pinned a Captain's rank on me and a chaplain's cross. We had, at long last after a five-year break in service, made it back into the active duty Army as a full-fledged chaplain.

Being stationed at the home of the Special Forces and airborne operations, I was given the opportunity to go to airborne school. I took my airborne physical and was sent to Fort Benning, Georgia, for training.

Once there, the doctor reviewing my records said, "Do you know you have a broken right leg?"

"No, I *used* to have a broken right leg. I broke it back in 2000."

"I'm looking at your X-rays. According to this, you still have a non-union of the right fibula."

"What?"

He clarified, "A broken leg."

Sure enough, my right leg was still cleanly broken, having never healed like the original docs thought it would. I was stamped as "non-airborne qualified" and returned to Ft. Bragg without wings. I was really sad but knew I was in the right place at the right time. The group that I was scheduled to train with had their first "burn-in" in over twenty years from a female Soldier whose chute failed to open. Because I was a chaplain, I was called out to do counseling with the Soldiers on the field and with the Rigger who had packed the parachute. Though it was no fault of his, he was still falling apart emotionally.

I ran with my sore right leg for years until I was finally given the opportunity to fix it again in 2008 at Brooke Army Medical Center (BAMC) in Fort Sam Houston, Texas. The doctors there evaluated my leg and said they could take a bone graph from my knee and stuff it into the break, and it would heal normally like it should have done years before. It would be a same-day surgery with a two-to-three day recovery. Jennifer was far more excited than I was. I think she was tired of me always using it as an excuse for not taking out the trash or standing long enough to wash the dishes or getting up to fix my own sandwich. "I have a broken leg" had become my favorite saying.

The nurse prepping me for surgery laughed as she looked at my chart. I asked what was so funny, and she said my chart said

I was scheduled to have my uterus removed. I asked her to kindly leave my uterus where it was, and she promised me she would as she went to get the proper chart. I medicinally fell asleep to the soothing sounds of "Keep Bleeding, Love" on the hospital speaker system and awoke to a world of stinging pain (and without a uterus).

The doctor came in to talk to me, and he said, "On the positive side, you have a very muscular leg."

I thanked him and asked the negative side.

He said, "I had to cut through a lot of muscle to get to the bone, so it's going to be at least a thirty-day recovery period with physical therapy to teach you to walk properly again."

I was at that time enrolled in a course called Clinical Pastoral Education (CPE) at Brooke Army Medical Center, and they had given me three day's recovery time, and any more than that would mean I would be dropped from the program. I came to work in a wheelchair, shaking and sweating from pain for weeks, even getting re-hospitalized once for the excessive pain.

At the end of the thirty days, the doctor looked at my new X-rays and announced confidently, "I believe it's actually gotten a little worse."

According to him, my leg had been so used to over compensating for the break that it had continued to do so, and the bone graph didn't take. Even to me the gap in the bone looked a little bit bigger than before on the X-rays. He put me on a permanent profile saying I would never run again. Knowing that would kill my military career, I pleaded for him to allow me to run at my own pace and distance. He agreed and wrote my permanent profile to read, "Run at own pace and distance," and then cautioned me that running too fast for too long could cause permanent damage.

It is now 2017. I run with a limp. It's not a very noticeable limp, I suppose, to anyone but me. I know it's there because it hurts. I've run with a limp for seventeen years now. I think it's because that's how long my leg has been broken.

RIOTOUS TRANSITION

When I was at Brooke Army Medical Center for my year of CPE, I was given the opportunity to attend Erskine Theological Seminary in Due West, South Carolina, to take classes toward a Doctorate of Ministry paid for by the Army. For two weeks we were flown to the sleepy town of Due West for classes, given three years worth of syllabuses, and taught how to write a doctoral dissertation. Throughout the rest of our time at BAMC, we could work on our college classes and submit them through the mail to the faculty at Erskine.

My advisor for my dissertation was a gentleman by the name of Dr. Lloyd Melton. As I and the other doctoral candidates sat in the classroom waiting for the good doctor to arrive, an older gentleman with long, shaggy white hair and overalls came in and collected the trash from the bin and left. When he returned a few minutes later, we all thought him to be the janitor, until he began teaching with his slow, relaxed Southern speech.

The greatest line I remember him saying was, "I have been a pastor for many years now, and I cannot stop people from putting me on a pedestal, but I can make it hell on them for trying to keep me there."

I like Dr. Melton a lot!

With my topic and title for my dissertation chosen, "Journaling as a Means to Spiritual Renewal (Help for the Compassion Fatigued)," I began throwing myself into finding ways to minister to my own battle weary soul and to the myriad of compassion-fatigued brothers and sisters in arms that I serve with in the military every day. The normal time for completing the doctorate program is three years. I was so passionate about the topic I'd chosen that I wrote the dissertation and received my doctoral degree before the year at Brooke Army Medical Center was over. The first thing I did after receiving my degree was to get on Facebook and write, "Dr. Pepper is a unique blend of twenty-three different flavors ... Trust me. I'm a doctor!"

So with a degree in hand and a year's worth of introspection completed since my first deployment to the life-altering planet of Iraq, my family and I PCSed (Permanent Change of Station) to Fort Leavenworth, Kansas. This is home to the Command General Staff College for all Majors hoping to become Lieutenant Colonels one day and home to the United States Disciplinary Barracks (USDB) for all Soldiers who commit crimes requiring long-term confinement.

It was here that a brand-new unit was being formed, the 40th Military Police Battalion. It was being created to run the disciplinary barracks so that the unit which had historically always run it, the 705th Military Police Battalion, could deploy to Iraq. I was given the great privilege of saying the first prayer the new Battalion heard. As a part of the ceremony, the 15th Military Police Brigade was being reconstituted to head the 705th and the newly formed 40th. This was historically important, because the 15th MP Brigade was the very first MP Brigade in the corps and had been inactivated for over thirty years!

Within the first few months of arriving, I became a part of

preparing the 705th for war, helping initiate the creation of the 40th Military Police Battalion, becoming a co-pastor to the inmates at the disciplinary barracks, being a part of the opening ceremonies for the newly built Joint Regional Correctional Facility (JRCF) for military offenses requiring shorter terms of confinement, and getting into full swing of the day-to-day ministry to Military Police officers and their families.

A typical week included Tuesday field trips with Soldiers to different locations throughout Kansas, pizza lunch Wednesdays with Soldiers in my office, Bible study nights in my home each Friday with a home-cooked meal, singles retreats, marriage retreats, sermons at the disciplinary barracks, and lots and lots of counseling, counseling, and more counseling.

Coming to an MP unit for the first time was strange and unfamiliar territory to me. I had spent my military career up to that point in a CSH (Combat Support Hospital) environment as a Protestant Father Mulchahy from the old TV series M.A.S.H. (Mobile Army Support Hospital). And suddenly there I was surrounded by Thirty-One Echoes and Bravos.

My education into their world began in a two-week preservice class in Ft. Leavenworth, Kansas. I looked around at the tired eyes of eighteen- and nineteen-year-old combat Veterans, most of whom had just arrived from Guantanamo Bay, Cuba, and I knew I had my work cut out for me.

From lockdown procedures to pepper spray and unarmed self-defense courses, I quickly realized that MPs are hands-on Soldiers. Each morning was spent running faster and farther than most deer, and each afternoon was filled with visiting MPs at the prison, Bible studies, marriage retreats, and multiple counseling sessions on every topic imaginable.

It was during these sessions that the rock-hard constitution of military justice took on the beating heart of wounded warriors. I heard stories of hurt and pain, of hope and disillusionment, of cracking or broken relationships, and saw tears from the fiercest fighters among our nation's ranks. I also listened awestruck to tales of heroism and valor that would shame Hollywood's attempt at capturing the heart of battle. I saw patriotism in its purest form pour out of youth day after day on a tiny chair in a little office over cups of too-strong coffee.

Soldiers constantly amaze me by raising their right hands to reenlist despite having already shed blood on their second and third deployments. I have read of a greatest generation. To this generation I tip my hat and respectfully say the bar has finally been raised.

I also grew to have great respect for the level of sincerity in the Christianity I saw expressed in the inmates at the disciplinary barracks. Those who came to church on Sunday needed no reminding that they were sinners, no reasons why they were in need of a Savior. None of them looked down their noses at the brown uniforms of the other churchgoers, and all of them prayed fervently for God's deliverance and mercy.

I often told the congregation at the Main Post Chapel that I knew the congregation in the USDB was praying for them every Sunday. I wrote the following poem to help articulate the respect I had grown to have for the inmate ministers who shared hope with the brand-new prisoners just arriving.

THE PREACHER CLOTHED IN BROWN

The preacher clothed in brown is a sinner, Son.
He doesn't preach in city pulpits or country towns.
The preacher clothed in brown is in prison, Son.
He's called by numbers instead of his name
by Soldiers making rounds.

What does the preacher wearing brown say, Dad?
Does he say he's sorry for what he's done?
What did the preacher wearing brown do, Dad?
To make him stay in prison even after his preaching's done?

The preacher wearing brown preaches Jesus, Son,
The same Jesus that your daddy preaches of.
The preacher wearing brown just did some sinning, Son,
But that sinning's been forgiven, just like ours by Jesus's love.

If his sins have been forgiven, Dad,
Then why's he still in prison, this preacher all in brown?
If his sins have been forgiven, Dad,
Shouldn't he be at home a sleepin', in comfort layin' down?

Even forgiven sins have consequences,
That need atoning for on earth.
But his slates been wiped clean by God, Son,
And that's what truly decides his worth.

I heard this preacher preachin', Son,
The Gospel plain and clear.
No fluff, no flowers, no tiptoein' in his message, Son
And all the men were payin' him attention there.

He told of Jesus's death and resurrection
This preacher clothed in brown,
Of heavenly judgment and acquittal
And of the Holy Spirit comin' down.

And as the preacher preached, Son,
His prison uniform of brown
It seemed to me transformed itself into a robe of white, Son
And on his head appeared a crown.

The preacher clothed in brown is a saint, Son.
The child of our Heavenly King.
The preacher clothed in brown is family, Son
Which makes him more precious than anything.

There is a preacher clothed in brown
But only to our eyes.
For Jesus sees him all in white
With eternity his prize.

There is a preacher clothed in brown
But only to our eyes.
Whom God Himself, will one day
Proudly recognize.

After an incredibly packed couple of months, the 40th received official notification that we would be deploying to Iraq in January of 2011. Life flew into fast-forward with preparations, classes, training, redeploying the 705th, retreats, and more counseling than I had done in all my months in Ft. Leavenworth up to that point combined.

I had deployed with medics before. I knew them and what they were capable of in chaotic situations. I had never served with MPs before. How would they react when the situation became dangerous and every decision counted? Well, one night I got the opportunity to set all my fears aside.

A class called the Army Corrections Academy was graduating on a Thursday night where I worked at the 40th Military Police Battalion. To celebrate, we were having a potluck at the Battalion around 1700 hours. I decided to just keep my uniform on for the function instead of changing after work.

Around 1900, things were wrapping up, and I headed home. Since my family was over at a friend's house watching the finale of *So You Think You Can Dance*, I was left to relax at home, although I stayed in uniform because our sister Battalion, the 705th MP Battalion, was returning from Iraq around midnight, and I planned on being there to greet them.

Around 1930, my wife called. "Did you know there is a riot down at the prison?"

No, as a matter of fact I didn't know that, and I was wondering how she did.

"Eileen's husband just got a call that inmates have taken over a portion of the prison and have a guard held hostage."

I was already in the car, racing toward the battalion headquarters before she finished her sentence.

On the way in, I called the Battalion Commander, Lieutenant Colonel Nelson, to see if she was aware of the situation.

"Hello, Chaplain. Yes, there is a situation here. It would be a good idea if you headed to the Battalion."

"I'm almost there, ma'am," I replied, already pulling up to the front of the building.

Two other Soldiers were running from their vehicles, attempting to get their berets on before they had to take them off again once they were inside. I managed a good chef hat look with mine before ripping it right back off and stuffing it in my cargo pocket.

Lieutenant Colonel Nelson was walking down the hall as I entered. "Good evening, Chaplain. Here's the situation. Apparently we have fourteen inmates who have taken over SHU (Specialized Housing Unit) East. They have roughed up the Correctional Specialist on duty, but he seems to be doing okay. They've allowed him to go into the shower area where he won't be assaulted anymore."

"Is anyone in there talking to them?" I asked.

"I don't think there is, Chaplain."

"I know all the inmates on that SHU. Can I try to talk to them?"

"That would be very helpful."

I sprinted back out of the building. In my vehicle I dialed Chaplain (Lieutenant Colonel) Jones, my supervisor, to see if he was already in route to the DB (disciplinary barracks). He hadn't received the news and was still at home. I recapped as quickly as I could while navigating the back roads to the military's largest prison. Twice the phone cut out, and I had to redial.

"I didn't get all of what you said, Chaplain Dicks, but I didn't like the sound of the parts I did hear."

I summarized, "We need you at the DB, Sir, quickly."

"Got it. I'm en route," he assured me.

By that time I was at the prison doing the race-the-beret-to-the-door game.

Command Sergeant Major Wallace was in the upper foyer of the facility on the cell phone with Command Sergeant Major Godwin, the DB command sergeant major. I badged in, went through a metal detector and two airtight bulletproof blast doors, and then was sprinting down the long hallway to the door that would take me to SHU East.

Opening the door and stepping in was like walking into the science fiction movie *Star Gate* because I had stepped through a portal into an entirely different world. The heat was oppressive, people were running back and forth, water was flowing over the cement floor, and the lights seemed to be dimmed. Soldiers were dressed in black riot gear, helmets, face shields, and body-length shields. I rounded yet another secure blast door and saw the riot glass windows that were the only thing separating me from fourteen frenzied inmates who had completely taken over their domain.

The once orderly SHU was flooded with water. Papers were scattered everywhere, and piles of soaked books littered the floor with other trash. The inmates had their shirts off or tied around their faces like bank robbers. Strutting back and forth like an angry hornet's nest that had been kicked, they were brandishing makeshift weapons, which looked all too lethal despite being homemade. Broken broomstick handles sharpened to a point. Metal legs from tables wielded like bats, the ends of which still had wicked-looking twisted metal pieces attached to them from where they had been ripped from their foundations. Unsolicited mental images assaulted me as to what would happen if one of those table legs made even a glancing contact with my skin.

"Hey, y'all, they sent in the chaplain!" I heard one of them scream, and everyone approached the glass.

"What's going on, guys? What are you doing, and what do you want?"

"We want Sergeant _____!" That's all we want. Send him down here!"

"Why do you want Sergeant ____?"

"He's been screwing with us for five days now, Chap. We been tellin' people, and nothing gets done, so we got to resort to this to get y'all's attention. It's a damn shame, but that's how it is."

Everyone was letting him talk; maybe this was the leader. I figured if he stood down there was a chance they all might.

"You've got our undivided attention right now. What do you want different?"

I scanned the room. There was a brown towel hanging from the wire mesh window of the shower. That's where the Correctional Specialist was being held hostage.

"What can I help make happen? Please give me something so this doesn't happen. You know if we come in there people are going to get hurt on both sides. That's not the way, brother. That's not how things get fixed. What do y'all want different?"

I could see he was considering when the second leader presented himself.

"No more talking. One-for-one exchange. Tell the chaplain. That's what we want, a one-for-one exchange."

The inmate, who was crouched down by a slit in the locked food tray door so we could hear each other, looked through the glass into my eyes and gave a slight shrug of his shoulders before speaking. "You heard him, one-for-one exchange. Send Sergeant _____."

Holy crap, I couldn't believe I was going to say this. I didn't believe there would ever come a time in my existence where I would actually have the opportunity or the slightest inclination to even want to consider saying this, but … "What about a one-for-one exchange with me? Send out the Correctional Specialist, and I'll come in."

He stared at me. I don't know if he didn't hear me or he didn't believe what he heard. Asking that question was too scary the first time. I prayed he didn't make me ask again.

"Hey, shut up, everybody!"

Instantly the armed mob behind him quieted.

"The chaplain just said something. What was that again, Chaplain?"

Crap. I was going to have to repeat it. I was scared to death, but I would honestly rather it had been me than the young Soldier sequestered in the shower. "Do a one-for-one exchange, me for the Specialist."

He stood up. "Chaplain wants to offer himself."

They huddled. Like a football team, they actually huddled to discuss it.

I was shaking, and I prayed, "Dear Jesus, don't let them see me shaking."

He came back. "Chaplain, we can't do it. We like you too much. No deal. Sergeant ____ or nobody. We want to talk to the Commandant and the Deputy Commandant."

"All right, I'll send for them."

As a side note, I had absolutely no idea that I had no right, ability, or authority to negotiate with inmates. Had they accepted my foolish suggestion I would have found out quickly enough that there was no way a door was being cracked open even slightly until the breach could be filled with up-armored, highly motivated

Military Police Officers on a mission to retrieve one of their own. In defense of my rapidly beating pulse however, I found this out only after the situation was contained. A weary Lieutenant Colonel Nelson was shaking her head and rubbing her eyes in exasperation. "What would make you think that would have been a good idea Chaplain?" I didn't have an answer which was probably for the best anyway.

A Soldier with a video camera disappeared to carry the inmates request to the Commandant.

The DOPs (Director Of Operations) officer who was over the prison came in and knelt beside me. As soon as the demands to talk to the Commandant were made, several inmates got shaving cream and smeared it over the top panes of glass. In order to see in one had to kneel in the water soaked floor and look through the lower panes.

The DOPs officer asked, "Who are the heavies [the leaders]?"

I pointed them out. Three different inmates had shown clear leadership within the group. He knocked on the glass and called for someone to talk to him. One of the inmates came and sat on a bench by the glass to talk.

The DOPs told me, "Keep an eye on the shower chaplain. Make sure the Specialist is okay."

So I watched the shower as he talked to the inmate.

One of the heavies yelled at the inmate, "I told you no more talking. Get away from there!"

So the inmate walked away. This happened several times. Every time an inmate approached the shower, we would knock on the glass and ask to talk to someone. This distracted them away from the Correctional Specialist. The DOPs officer asked one of them how the Specialist was doing and was told he was bruised but not hurt too badly.

A second gentleman in civilian clothes knelt down beside me, extended his hand to shake mine, and said, "I'm the hostage negotiator. I hear you've been doing a good job talking to them. What's going on?"

I explained what I knew up to that point, showed him where the hostage was being held, what kind of weapons were being wielded, who the bosses were, and their general complaint.

"Good job, Chaplain. I'm going to take it from here."

Relief washed over me and then an instant feeling of guilt. I'm not sure why I felt guilty for being relieved. I just know that's what I felt.

I walked back around the corner. There were two sets of black-garbed storm troopers in two columns down two hallways that intersected. The Soldiers stretched back as far as I could see down each hallway. Shields, helmets, shotguns with nonlethal rounds and suddenly, by comparison, the inmates didn't seem all that intimidating at all. Orders were being given down each line—points of entry, snatch-and-grab teams, shield bearers, the biggest and strongest up front. Not a single glint of fear in any eye, just adrenaline and focus.

When all the directions seemed to have been given, I asked, "Can I get your attention for a second?"

"Shut up! Chaplain's talking!"

Instant silence.

"Let's pray. Dear God, protect these Soldiers. Get them in, and get them out safely. Protect our brother being held, and let everybody go home safe tonight. In your name I pray …"

At least fifty "amen's" sounded in unison, and it felt like a bass speaker rumbling in my chest.

I was holding open the door so they could rush past into the breach, each Soldier holding on to the back of the body armor of the Soldier in front of them. I slapped the front plate of each person's body armor as they shuffled past me into the chaos.

"The Lord bless you, the Lord bless you, the Lord bless you ..." to each as they passed.

After all of them went by, I was staring at Sergeant Laduron and two other medics who were steeling themselves to take casualties.

Sergeant Laduron and I had deployed together for fifteen months in Iraq with the 28th Combat Support Hospital during OIF 06-08. I knew what a professional he was in the midst of blood, carnage, and suffering. He was no less so this night.

Pop! Pop! Pop!

Screams echoed above the shouting. I could hear coughing and sneezing, and suddenly my face was beginning to burn as well. OC Spray ... nasty stuff, even in residual. I started coughing and sneezing, trying to clear my eyes as my collar and skin started stinging like they were on fire. Two Soldiers in riot gear came sprinting toward me, and between them was a battered but happy looking kid ... the hostage.

They rushed past me to round a corner and headed down the hallway to the gym, which had been converted into a makeshift casualty collection point for patients. Three more battle-dressed Soldiers burst through the hallway. They were carrying an inmate like a human battering ram, his arms flex-cuffed behind him, unconscious, head drooped down, pouring out blood from multiple lacerations. I put my arms under one of his shoulders and helped bear his weight down the hallway to the gym, leaving a bright-red trail behind us all the way down the hall.

On the ground, although I was still in the gym, I was suddenly back in Iraq. I stabilized the inmate's head with my hands while at the same time scanning his body for other injuries. His left ear was almost completely severed, dangling by a small slice of skin. I tried not to focus on the fact that I could see way too far into his head through the two puncture wounds above his left eye. He began to moan in response to pain but would not open his eyes or show any other sign that he could hear us.

Sergeant Laduron started his IV and put in a nasal breathing tube with the aid of a paramedic from the fire department. Being at the head, I gave the "one, two, three, lift!" count as the patient was placed on a backboard and strapped down. I helped as he was lifted onto the stretcher. He was wheeled away, and I turned to other casualties, which had poured in since I had first entered the gym.

The liberated hostage was sitting in a folding chair with officers talking to him, comforting him. At least six new inmate casualties were scattered around the gym with Correctional Specialists surrounding each of them. I saw Chaplain Jones, Chaplain Morris, and Chaplain Wilkins kneeling beside different clusters of Soldiers and casualties, talking, praying, laying comforting hands on shoulders, smiling, and doing awesome ministry. I'm still proud of them, proud to have been on their team.

I saw a water fountain and then looked again at the Soldiers and inmates alike, all covered in blood and sweat and panting from their ordeal. I asked Chaplain Jones if we could get cups from the chapel section for water. He said he had already unlocked everything for that very purpose. The next hour or so consisted of a thousand trips to the water fountain filling cups and taking them to the grateful Soldiers, as well as kneeling before the cuffed inmates and pouring water in their mouths for them. They were as grateful for it as the Soldiers.

"Thank you, Chaplain," I heard one of the inmates say.

A few minutes before he had been waving a metal bat of

death, screaming for blood. Now he was respectfully telling me how grateful he was for a simple Styrofoam cup of water.

"Chaplain, one of the inmates is asking for you by name in the SHU."

I went back to where, only a few hours ago, I had been doing hostage negotiations, scared to death. This time I was on the other side of the glass. The floor was a battlefield, blood in huge puddles, more trash, torn clothes, and rubber pellets all over the floor. I picked up two of the rubber BBs to remind myself of the evening and then headed to the cell of the relocked-down inmate requesting to see me.

"Chaplain—" He was choked up, and I could tell he was trying not to cry. "This took me back to Iraq, Chaplain. I lost three of my men in '06 in Iraq. I was doing good, but this just brought it all back."

I was in Iraq in '06. We were both Soldiers there at the same time. Now he was an inmate, and we both shared our PTSD from different sides of a locked cell.

Back outside, with the pictures completed by MPI for the inevitable upcoming investigations, cleaning had begun in earnest. It was necessary to get up some of the human biohazard soaking the facility, and the Soldiers coming on duty for their shifts that night were filtering through to help with cleanup.

I heard the First Sergeant slap a young Soldier's riot chest plate and say, "Welcome to your first day with the United States Army Corrections, Private!"

A lot of laughter from the surrounding Soldiers and even a little applause as the young Soldier, who didn't look big enough to even fit into the riot gear, beamed from ear to ear.

I walked back to the chaplains' office and did some much-needed debriefing with Chaplain Jones and the Chaplain

Assistant, Sergeant Tanner. I discovered that Chaplain Wilkins had gone to the hospital to be with the patients. After handshakes, words of affirmation, and comfort, I headed out of the DB. It was two o'clock in the morning, and I ached all over.

Driving home, I saw all of the Command teams' vehicles in the Battalion parking lot, so I turned in and parked. Walking slowly from sheer emotional more than physical exhaustion, I climbed the stairs to the main floor and headed to the TOC (Tactical Operations Center). Inside were Lieutenant Colonel Nelson, Major Locke, Major Robinson, Sergeant Major Breckenridge, Command Sergeant Major Wallace, and others.

These were the Soldiers I would deploy with back to Iraq in only a few months. Each of them acquitted themselves well that night; everyone orchestrated the chaos in their world like master conductors. I don't have the right words to convey my pride in their professionalism, resolve, and heroic actions. They are my heroes.

I don't know why I always get to hang around such heroic people, but things have an interesting way of falling into place, and I have had the awesome privilege of being numbered among the friends of incredible people. The greatest of which, in my world, was waiting for me at home even if it was then nearing three in the morning.

I walked into my bathroom at home, stripped, showered, and then scrubbed blood out of my ACUs for the next fifteen minutes, more as a cleansing of my soul than for my uniform, and then collapsed into the safest spot in the whole world, the arms of my greatest hero ... my wife, whose very presence made it all right to finally fall asleep. Wow, what a night.

SPACE ANGELS AND
TOOTH FAIRIES

Female fighters. I tell you what, there is something incredibly attractive about a sidearm on swaying hips. But don't get the wrong impression. These females are as deadly as the male Soldiers around them. More so in some cases simply because you may not be expecting the level of ferocity and fight they can bring to an engagement when called upon to do so.

I almost feel sorry for the unsuspecting civilian male at a club back on earth who fails to realize the beautiful young knockout he is going to attempt to sexually harass has been trained in more combative techniques than he's ever seen on television. With such training she has the ability to pretzel his little hurt pride into submission, or if need be, to take the life right out of his big, blue, surprised eyes. Black widow is way too harsh ... but the metaphor isn't entirely without merit. Mainly I think of them like they are: space angels.

The manual for hope I always carry with me says, "Are not all angels ministering spirits sent to serve those who will inherit salvation?" (Hebrews 1:14, NIV). Everywhere we go, there is a group, tribe, race, or species that needs saving. Into the dirt, gravel, heat, trash, pain, and sorrow infecting the various war-torn planets in this universe come the most beautiful women in the entire galaxy. They bring hope, salvation, and a sense of grace to an otherwise chaotic, senseless suffering. They bring justice, order, and a graceful sense of beauty everywhere their small-sized boots march. They are by definition angels, and they all smell better than me.

There are three particular space angels that I fell head over combat-booted heels, completely and hopelessly devoted to on that second deployment. They are among the closest friends I will ever have in my life, and for a joiner, that number tends to be very low. I mean, we have thousands of acquaintances and defacto family members, all of whom we would willingly lay our lives down for if called upon to do so, but the "one time blonde now brunette iPhone-wielding bombshell," the "exotic English is my second language El Salvadorian Chief," and the "Etta James lookalike quickest wit in the western quadrant" are bona fide space angels. They became my three slices of heaven in an otherwise hellish environment.

First Lieutenant promotable Camille Acred is the beautiful pin-up picture she had better never find you have. As the Deployment Sexual Assault Response Coordinator (DSARC), she tended to take sexual harassment very seriously. Sergeant First Class Ford often says that he watched with his own two eyes as she shot a man in the face at seventy-five meters for "good gaming" an unsuspecting female Soldier. I don't know if the story is true, but I have no real reason to doubt it either.

Serving in the operations section, First Lieutenant Acred kept her finger on the pulse of the unit and eyes glued to the latest texts on her iPhone. She was always aware of who was moving where, when, and with how many armed escorts. She is hard working, naturally cheerful, and always finding the best possible ways to care for her Soldiers. She's the first to lend a helping hand or swift kick to the appropriate region of those who need one. On more than one occasion, I found myself uncomfortably close to the blast area when she switched from guardian to avenging angel, completely annihilating the incompetent behavior of this or that fellow Soldier who made the fatal mistake of thinking girls are nicer. She's my hero, and being level two Combatives Instructor qualified, she could also be my body guard.

Chief Warrant Officer Two Sandra Chugan is my dark-haired, built-in tan, permanently affixed smile, El Salvadorian expert in all things property related. There is not a bolt in the space craft that brought us to that sand dune that Chief Chugan did not have accounted for on a hand receipt that she had personally double-checked and committed to memory. Known for her infectious laugh, which can be heard several rooms away from wherever she is, rooms tend to brighten when she walks in and then give a collective sigh of sadness when she leaves.

I tried to run a race with her one time, thinking how nice it would be to take a leisurely jog for a few miles, talk, laugh, and cross the finish line together. She began the race with me and then ended up waiting at the finish line to cheer me on a good fifteen minutes before the finish line even came into my sight, and I have excellent vision. She has always cheered me on, even though it's my job as joiner to do the cheering.

Master Sergeant Teresa Watson will forever be the fastest wit in the western quadrant, and arguably much farther than that. Her weapon needs never be drawn as she shoots down myriads of uncomprehending victims who unwisely place themselves in her sights through some unfortunate word or deed that is not up to par with universal common sense. I was surprised every day by how often, and how many people, threw themselves into her firing lane of vicious intelligence, sharply articulated, for the most ridiculous of reasons. A half smile and incredibly high-arched eyebrow would signal the chambering of a round as clearly as any rifle bolt.

Just as swiftly, bullets of pure irony, cased in polished sarcasm, fired toward doomed targets. They never saw the flash before being brought down by her barrage of merciless turns of phrase and clear statements of the painfully obvious that the rest of us were too slow, or too polite, to point out. She has a kindred heart to mine without the burdensome hassle of a joiner's conscience. She makes me smile.

There are angels whom God created before mankind that are tasked with helping us mere mortals out. But space angels smell nicer, look nicer, and by their very presence give me a level of motivation to excel that I'm sure I would not otherwise have on deployments. In fact, without space angels, I doubt I would ever see the inside of a gym on distant planets.

It is a cosmic fact that soda-bellies are never frowned upon by other soda-bellied males. As it is, there is something mysterious and magical about working alongside the prettier versions of the universes fiercest fighters. In multiple solar systems, they have become myth and legend. It's kind of like getting to go to work with the tooth fairy.

By the way, please don't scoff when I talk about the tooth fairy because she will always be welcome in my house. Each time a tooth is lost in my home, whichever one of my four children have lost it, immediately becomes the focus of attention in the house. Why? Because they know that sometime that night the tooth fairy will silently sneak into their rooms and replace the tooth they've got with some money! Oh, their eyes light up! Big toothless smiles, imaginations run wild with the magical and wonderful world of the Tooth Fairy, Santa Claus, and Easter Bunny. And the world is a fun and exciting place to be.

There have been nights when I have tiptoed into my children's room to find the plastic baggy with a tooth inside not under the pillow but clutched desperately to the chest of my sleeping child, who tried so hard to stay awake and get a peek at the tooth fairy. It's nights like that when the tooth fairy tends to get her directions mixed up, and she brings the money and slips it under Mommy and Daddy's pillow on accident.

The following morning my children will shake their heads, hands on their hips, and say, "Did that silly tooth fairy get lost *again*?"

Now tell me honestly. Who wouldn't want to live in a world like that?

I am a Christian. I don't place my Lord Jesus in the same fantasy world as the tooth fairy. Jesus is very much alive and real. And I teach my children that Jesus is a living, real part of our family's lives. I have been told that allowing my children to believe in the tooth fairy will make them throw out Jesus and angels and spiritual realities once this world rips the tooth fairy away from them and replaces her face with that of a well-meaning Mom and Dad. But I think God gives children a heart of imagination and wonder, hearts that poets and dreamers struggle and strain to remember. For a period of time the world is magical and wonderful and mysterious.

I have journeyed thousands of miles away from my precious children. Where I have walked I have seen children who looked back at me with ancient and tired eyes. They had no childlike deceptions of a world that is good. No Santa Claus, no money for their lost teeth from the tooth fairy. They lived in a world where death and destruction were their neighbors.

IED was an acronym that needed no explanation as they had ripped childhood away from them so early in life. I saw children that were experts at asking for money from foreign Soldiers—not for candy, not for toys, but for food for their families. I journeyed to a land without children, just tiny adults who knew better than most of the world the harshness and the stark reality of this all too non-magical world. I saw them, and I longed to see the tooth fairy in their eyes, but she did not live there.

She does, however, still live in the hearts of four little angels in a tiny home in the United States. In that house is wonder and mystery and magic and excitement and love. And maybe one day when I am old and God has granted me back the mind and heart of a child, the tooth fairy will again sneak into my room wearing the face of one of my precious children and perhaps she will slip a dollar bill under my pillow in exchange for one of my few remaining teeth. And I shall awake the next morning filled with excitement and wonder in a world that is good. Yes, the tooth fairy will always be welcome in my house.

Until I get back to that house, however, I will suck in my gut, run an extra mile, avoid the fried food section of the DFAC, and purposely add bass to my voice as a sign of masculinity while in the presence of the sweetest, meanest eye rollers in the galaxy. There may or may not ever be a marble monument engraved with the names of legendary heroines that I have had the privilege to serve beside, but their names will ever be written on the tablet of my heart. Colonel Ruth Lee, Captain Maria Ortiz, Captain Susan Stankorb, Captain Lisa Paroz, First Sergeant Nichole Haines, Staff Sergeant Jamie

Misplay, Lieutenant Colonel Erica Nelson, First Sergeant Shannon Altamirano, First Lieutenant Camille Acred, Chief Warrant Officer Two Sandra Chugan, Master Sergeant Teressa Watson—beautiful, dangerous, and deadly—but worth it. Space angels.

SHRUNK TO A NUB

Sergeant First Class Ford loves cigars. In fact, he is one of the few people I have ever met that can be called a cigar connoisseur. When Sergeant First Class Ford arrived on the strange planet of Iraq, he was very quickly made the president of the local cigar club. This in and of itself is not surprising because, while attending one of the smoky meetings of this club, Sergeant First Class Ford was asked why cigars have paper bands on them. Without pausing, he gave an informative lecture on how Mary Queen of Scotts loved cigars but would not let her hand touch tobacco. Because she was uncomfortable using only one glove to handle the cigar, her advisors wrapped a small band of paper around it so she could grasp the cigar bare fingered without sullying her royal digits. A shining example of why he is cigar club president worthy.

What surprised me is that Sergeant First Class Ford informed me he wanted to have me knighted as the vice president of the cigar club. (I think it's because I had pledged to be a supplier of cigars, not because I know anything about them, but hey, vice president sounds pretty cool, and no, vice presidents never get too much media attention unless they shoot someone on a hunting trip, which was not my plan at the time.)

One night I was headed back to my room after a rigorous workout and a hasty dinner when I noticed a gathering of said cigar club around a community table outside, and I decided to walk over and join them. Sergeant First Class Ford was regaling the crowd with several cigar-related adventures from previous deployments.

When he saw me, his face lit up like his bright cigar, and he asked, "Chaplain! What kind of cigar would you like?"

As a potential candidate for vice presidency, I didn't want to say, "I have no idea what brands of cigars exist," so instead I diplomatically asked, "What kinds do you have?"

He rattled off several to the ooos and ahhs of the listening group. After he had listed the Baskin-Robbins 31 flavors and all eyes turned expectantly to me, I was in no better shape than I was before to make a choice.

It was similar to being at a fancy French restaurant, trying to impress my French friends by ordering from a French menu and not knowing French, having no idea what the waiter had just spouted off as choices.

So I answered as smoothly as possible, "Why doesn't the president let me try his favorite?"

All smiles and nods from the group for a decision well made. I knew I was a shoo-in for the office. Proof that idiots do sometimes get hired to political positions, I suppose.

You see, cigars not only have different names, but different levels of strength or death-like effect producing potency in non-very rarely smoking individuals such as myself, and I had unwisely just asked a smoking expert, who had spent years building up an immunity to iocane powder, to give me his favorite dosage of the stuff.

He reached into his treasure box and gingerly lifted, with two tenderly cradling hands, his cigar of choice. I am certain a light emanated from the humidor as he did so and an unseen choir began singing as he reverently handed me his version of the Holy Grail.

"This ... is a Nub, Chaplain." He waited expectantly, so I quickly changed my face to a look of awe, which I assumed to be appropriate for the situation. For the sake of the other less informed members of the cigar club, he explained the Nub. (I listened in a non-interested manner as though this was common knowledge.) He said in cigar shops people will smoke their cigars so that the Queen of Scotts' cigar band label can be seen by all. If I am smoking a cheap cigar, I shall be shunned. If I am smoking a Rolex equivalent banded cigar, people will gravitate toward me as though King Arthur had returned. All eyes turned back to me now, wide as though I was King Arthur suddenly made manifest. After all, it was I who held aloft the Excalibur of cigars ... the fabled Nub.

In order to light the said cigar, Sergeant First Class Ford lit a long match, and I had to draw vigorously several times to make sure the flame took. It was then I realized my fatal mistake. I had just drawn into my mouth riot control strength CS Gas and had to look at my adoring fans (or at least the cigar's adoring fans) and let out a convincing, "Ahhh."

I wanted to cough and scream out, "Ahhh sh**!" run back into the barracks, and inhale the fire extinguisher, which I'm sure would have been an improvement to my lungs. However, as this would not have been appropriate for a potential vice president of the cigar club (let alone for a chaplain), I smiled and wheezed slowly out, "Ahhh," and left the rest hanging in the air like a dangling modifier for my upcoming nightmares.

The next hour saw us slowly drawing down the cigar's length.

It was taking as long as the troop draw down in the Middle Eastern star system. The club policy was no one was allowed to leave the table until everyone had finished their cigars.

When Sergeant First Class Ford spoke to First Lieutenant Acred as she started to leave for the bathroom thirty minutes into the adventure, saying, "I know you're not leaving yet. Chaplain and I still have cigars left," I knew I was doomed to my fate. I made witty banter while the planet began to spin, casually wiped away beads of sweat, and thanked the Lord for the cover of night so that my greenish pallor could be hidden.

Finally we excused ourselves, and I stumbled gracefully to my room, turned off the lights, collapsed on my bed, and held on with two hands so I didn't fall off the spinning planet. At two o' clock in the morning, I finally woke up with the taste of Nub fresh on my breath and the realization that I was still fully clothed … and an idiot.

I could almost hear God smile and say, "Want another one, son?"

UNSEEN BADGES

Even in laughter the heart may be sad.
Proverbs 14:13

Messages take a while to travel through space, but once they arrive, they can sometimes hurt more than a slap in the face. I can see it now, a young troop who has been waiting for strangely delayed mail for months finally gets (instead of a big care box) a single card in a plain envelope. Still, excited for some correspondence, and now with the hope that more is on the way, he opens his coveted treasure in the presence of his buddies, who are all hoping that it's not what they think it is.

I wish that just as he unseals the flap, a huge hand could erupt from the paper and slap him hard across the face. Yeah ... that would be cool. Harsh maybe, but not as harsh as a one paragraph, politely vague explanation, for why the valued relationship is now in the past. It would also help the stander-bys to recognize the signs and symptoms of a battle buddy who will be in shock for the next mission because of a traumatic brain injury from a giant slapping hand in the mail. Truth in advertising. This letter says, "I hate you, and I hurt you." Yep, mail like that breeds hope. Hope each one I open doesn't have a great big hand in it ready to slap me.

I laugh a lot. Most Soldiers I know laugh a lot.

Dave Roever, a motivational Christian speaker who was horribly wounded serving as a Navy SEAL on an obscure jungle planet once said, "I beat back depression one laugh at a time."

I spend a lot of my time as a joiner laughing with Soldiers, drinking coffee, talking about extremely insignificant things, often in inappropriate ways, as they decelerate and defuse from unseen pressures that would crush softer souls. They seem to bear up under the weight with the strange help of the many calluses military life has earned them, but it seems the harder the pressure, the more necessary the laughter. The times I sit and laugh about nothing in an undemanding, nonjudgmental manner, tends invariably to somehow earn me the right to later sit on sacred ground with those same Soldiers and hear stories that wrench all laughter away from me.

I have noticed a pattern among the warriors of our time. Broken relationships laughed at hours before are wept over in private conversation. Nightmares that are held at bay only by the body refusing to go to sleep. Barely contained, almost uncontrollable anger at the slightest provocation (usually dealing with mundane issues that were once easily overlooked). Addictions from sleep aides to smoking to drinking to a host of others to drown out reality at all cost. They struggle with every bit of fight within them to avoid becoming zombies inside, living but dead, with each day being nothing but a gray haze of survival. Young men and women on their third, fourth, even fifth deployments, and yet they serve with pride.

These scars they bear are unseen badges earned by sacrifice to a planet that loves them but is filled with people that don't understand them. How does one explain, for instance, that feeling alone while in a crowd is the saddest feeling but one I wouldn't trade for anything? I wouldn't lose that feeling because it was purchased by huddling together in instantly over-crowded bunkers with other wide-eyed, ridiculously grinning Soldiers while being attacked at two in the morning. The crowd of Soldiers that shared my terror were lost to the pages of yesterday's war, and now I find myself lonely in crowds yet unwilling to have the unseen badge taken from me at any price. But how do you explain that to those who haven't been there?

So we laugh ... I found myself at Camp Liberty at a sister cigar club to Camp Cropper's as a host of Soldiers I had never met laughed at relationship pains and failed coping mechanisms. We shared badges, which each of us could see and understand plainly. We felt camaraderie from the shared knowledge that we were the only ones who could see them, and that was okay.

I remember on my prior mission walking through the hospital and checking on staff and patients. One particular week I saw Soldiers who had been horribly mangled by IEDs and mortars. Tubes flowed from every artery and opening, and what wasn't tubed was covered in gauze. Room after room, it was the same until I saw an individual on a bed with nothing more than a breathing tube. He had no visible bruises, breaks, or punctures. His eyes were closed in peaceful sleep, and the machine method-ically kept rhythm for his breathing. After a few days, I began to see the results of multiple surgeries; the gauze began coming off, breaks were set, and healing, and sleeping Soldiers were awake, smiling and laughing with brothers and sisters in arms. I noticed as well that the sleeping man was missing.

I assumed he had awakened and gone home, so I asked a nurse about him. She said he had died during the night. I was truly surprised. All of the horrific injuries I had seen on the other Soldiers had mended, and yet the one who died had seemed fine to me. Out of curiosity I asked what had happened to him. The nurse said he had been standing too close to the blast area when an IED had detonated. Although he had no puncture wounds, the concussive blast had liquefied many of his internal organs, and he died from untreatable, unseen internal injuries.

I tell that story to show that many of the Soldiers I serve with are suffering from unseen internal injuries. Merely being too close as loved ones were killed in combat, too close to friends and family who were ripped away before their time, has left internal injuries as deadly as any caused by bullets or shrapnel. I myself have found that I have strange quirks that I didn't have before. For instance, whenever I am in the bathroom, I try to never look into the mirror when I'm washing my hands. After realizing I was literally scared to look in the mirror, I did some personal reflection to discover why. Here's what I discovered.

I like Spades. I don't play Hearts, and Poker cost money. But Spades, now that's a game of strategy and teamwork that I can really relax with. In fact, I relaxed to it every night around 8:00 p.m. in a little building by the hospital we called McKay Mansion. The normal crew consisted of myself, Mark Bivins (the hospital First Sergeant), my battle buddy Captain Darryl Metcalf (our Patient Administration Division officer), Captain John Green (the Supply officer), and Lieutenant Colonel Andy Lankowicz (the Deputy Commander for the hospital). One of us normally sat on the sidelines heckling, waiting for our turn to rotate into the next game while the other four battled it out at the table.

Females don't need games to talk. They get together sometimes for the specific purpose of just talking—about their feelings, emotions, and stressors from the day, and laughing and supporting each other. It's all very straightforward, all very healthy. That, however, is not how the male species gets things done. There must be some sort of distractor or another reason for talking. Ours happened to be Spades.

As cards flew, events of the day were rehashed. As "books" were made, concerns got aired and dealt with. If ever things began to get a little too emotional, a well-aimed, well-timed flatulent outburst kept the appropriate level of testosterone and manliness flowing in the room so no one felt too girlish about expressing their inner thoughts and feelings. The end result tended to be a healthy, albeit stinky, room of comfort where men were able to openly decompress from stressful days in a hospital in the middle of a war on an alien planet.

It was in the middle of this nightly ritual one evening when our game was silenced with a call that there was an anticipated high volume of patients inbound to the hospital, a mass cal event. In a heartbeat, the room turned from laughter to all business. Card hands that had been greedily guarded from straying eyes of the opponent players were carelessly left unguarded, and the room still echoing from laughter lay empty as its former occupants sprinted toward the hospital, steeling themselves for what they were about to see.

The news was quickly passed down that there was another bombing in the Tal Afar cluster, and there were already thirty dead with over a hundred wounded. Since we had only a sixteen-bed hospital, Captain Metcalf who was in charge of patient movement got on the phone to tell the incoming birds we could only accept fifteen people. I put on a pair of gloves, got cutting scissors, and got in line in the triage area in front of the hospital, waiting for the patients to arrive. I would be assisting in cutting off all clothing so they could be thoroughly examined simultaneously for weapons and wounds before entering the hospital.

The fire department arrived to help as extra litter bearers, and I was given my assistant, John Green, and a civilian contractor as my cut team. I instructed the other three on the procedures for clearing the patients when they came in. Then we waited. Fifteen minutes out. Five minutes out. Twenty minutes out.

"Stand down. The patients have been diverted to Striker instead of us."

Adrenaline drained. We returned to McKay to finish a now half-hearted game and called it an early night at 11:00 p.m.

I had just got into a good sleep when the radio by my bed screamed me into a conscious state. "Attention on the net. Mass cal! I say again, mass cal! All personnel report to the hospital immediately!"

I leapt out of bed, hastily dressed in a PT uniform, and bolted out of the door into the darkness. Running by the First Sergeant and Captain Green's rooms, I banged on their doors just in case they hadn't heard the radio. They hadn't. Lights came on.

Sleepy and slightly annoyed heads poked out at the same time, looking like, "You better have something important to say."

I summarized, "Mass cal!"

Sleep instantly dissolved from their faces as they disappeared back inside their rooms, reappearing seconds later like Supermen from their respective phone booths, and the sprint was on once again.

Gloves on, scissors ready, scrub top over the PT shirt, teams aligned, five minutes out. Twenty critically wounded patients inbound for our sixteen-bed hospital! New reports saying one hundred and seventy-five dead, over two hundred wounded. Birds were on the ground. First litter rushed in front of me. I leaned over to begin cutting off combat boots to discover no boots, only two tiny little feet. Not a Soldier, a four-year-old little boy with his head completely open to God and everyone else. I let the others cut as I applied a gentle cup with my hands around his head to stabilize it until it could be immobilized.

I suddenly realized by the warmth spilling through my fingers that I was the only thing holding his insides inside his head.

I went with the stretcher into the ER and maintained the hold until I was relieved by a doctor, who said, "Say a prayer, Chaplain."

I did. I whispered a barely audible one and was startled by multiple voices echoing amen with me.

Back outside, a million bodies, it seemed, were dancing and swirling around each other, cutting clothes, checking vitals, shouting orders—a rhythmic, orderly kind of chaos. There were more children than I could count, broken bodies of parents, elderly women fighting against me as I tried to cut off the last vestiges of their modesty so they could be seen inside.

"Hurry, Chaplain. We need to get her inside now."

I laid aside the scissors and used my hands to rip open her dress and was left feeling as violated as I'm sure she felt herself.

"Good job, go!"

She was inside. More were wheeled toward me.

The first wave was done. A second was on its way in fifteen minutes. I scanned the scene and saw the civilian contractor sitting on the ground, a thousand-yard stare in his eyes, dried tear streaks on his face. I told myself to remember to talk to him later. The dark-soaked remnants of shredded clothes were strewn everywhere on the ground. I began picking them up and putting them in biohazard bags as others hosed down the stretchers and rickshaws in preparation for the next salvo.

"Chaplain, we need you in here!"

I ran into the ER and saw every spot filled with people working on the wounded. Litters with casualties lined the hallways of the hospital outside the ER. I saw another little boy being worked on, and he was fighting with all his might while the nurse tried in vain to get an IV in.

I held down both of his legs with my right arm and held his arms with my left, struggling to keep him still so the nurse could work. The boy was probably five or six years old with a gaping head wound similar to the other child's, but he was yelling something in Arabic. All I could make out was the Arabic word for mommy.

I leaned my face toward his ear and softly began singing "Hush Little, Baby, Don't You Cry."

I teared up as he stopped crying and focused on my face and voice.

"Keep singing, Chaplain," I heard the nurse say as the IV was successfully started.

I sung to him until I realized his chest was no longer rising and falling. I began to say something, but the doctor was way ahead of me.

"Intubate, he's not breathing."

And just like that they were breathing for him.

As they worked on him, I allowed myself to be crowded out of the way so they could get elbow room to work. They were packaging everyone they could to fly out to Dahuk where there was a neurosurgeon. The DSC (deep space Chinook) was expected to be on the ground ready to take almost all of them within one hour. Not a lot of time. I went from bed to bed, praying with patients and staff, and then worked my way back outside to find the contractor.

I sat down next to him and offered him a Gatorade and a listening ear.

"How can people do this to children?" he asked.

I had no answer. I don't think he wanted one.

A nurse knelt down beside me, whispering in my ear, "Chaplain, we need you inside. One of the little boys with the head injury just died."

I rushed inside, wove through the litters of the freshly bandaged wounded, and worked my way back to the ICU ward. There was the little boy I had sung to. But he was still breathing!

I know I looked confused at the nurse, because she said, "Not this one. He's doing really well. It's another child."

I was led to the back, where the first child I had seen off the bird lay in silent death. I lay my hand on his bandaged head and prayed for his family, the hospital staff, and all who were still fighting for their lives. Then I slowly closed the young boy's eyes.

I helped to wash his body and whispered, "Good night, little brother," as they sealed him in the black bag and awaited mortuary affairs to come and take him away.

The next wave landed to the same blur of action, pain, and heroic efforts on the part of the hospital staff. A third wave came shortly after that to the same effect. Due to the amazing skill and determination of my fellow Soldiers, the one little boy was the only life lost in the hospital that night. The rest were successfully loaded onto a DSC and spirited away to their best possible chance of survival in this world. A lot of hugs, handshakes, meaningful looks of admiration and concern from everyone. I stood amidst the noblest of our nation—the heroes of our time, those that history will record with nostalgic awe—and I could not and still cannot begin to express my pride in them.

So tired we could barely walk (it was already 5:00 a.m.), I shook the hands of Darryl, Mark, Andy, and John before we turned to leave and collapse inside our rooms. I said, "Spades, tonight, eight o'clock?"

They each smiled and said, "We'll be there."

And they were. We needed the laughter and safety to decompress—and the smelly safe haven that helps heal the healers.

I woke up screaming—images of small children singing lullabies with their heads split open still dancing before my eyes. In my dream, I was covered in blood. I couldn't get it off of my uniform or my hands. Sweating and heart racing I rolled out of bed, stumbled out of my CHU, and headed toward the bathroom. I turned on the sink and splashed water on my face, trying to wake up from the nightmare.

Blood mixed into the water, pouring down the drain. I jerked my eyes up to the mirror to see a scared face covered in streaks of blood and a blood-soaked uniform. I jumped back from the mirror in the midst of a panic attack until I collected myself enough to remember I had gone straight from the chaos in the ER to collapsing on my bed without ever bathing or even taking off my uniform. To this day I hesitate before looking into the mirror, afraid of what I will see. This is just one of my unseen badges. I have many. Most of my brothers and sisters in arms have more, and I love them for it.

A SOLDIER'S LIFE

Ever forward, never back
Hold the line, mustn't crack
Stitch the wound, staunch the flow
Say good-bye, let him go

A Soldier's life is hard.

Fill the void night and day
Make the memories go away
Pretend to be the man you were
Keep the lie away from her

A Soldier's life is hard.

When the day is done
The battle won
And homeward march we all
No enemy could make us flee
But the insane sanity
Of mundane mediocrity
Makes even the mighty among us fall.

But I'd take the hardened Soldier's life
This truth I know too well
Over the daily grind
Of civilian strife
To a Soldier a life without war is hell.

A Soldier's life is hard.

These are the wounds that I have earned
I scribble down my lessons learned
On a page for all to see
I write in verse
And bless my curse
A Soldier's life for me.

A Soldier's life is hard
But it's that hardened life
With all its strife
That keeps America free.

A Soldier's life is hard
but it's the only life for me.

NEBUCHADNEZZARED

There's something about a good alien food story and what it did to your insides that's just worth retelling over and over again. Every Veteran has them. Either it was the alien water or something eaten on the market that caused a biblical proportioned Armageddon within their intestines, but the fact that they survived to tell about it makes it worth hearing and telling repeatedly to any and everyone who might accidentally listen.

My first off-world beloved culinary masterpiece story happened in South Korea. It was a twelve-month unaccompanied tour to a nearby planet that our fathers had fought and died on in years past. One of their delicacies was a dish called Kaygogee. It was dog meat. I ate it just to get the privilege of telling people in the future that I had done it. What I couldn't finish I took home in a doggy bag for later.

My trip with the 28th was no exception. After a long day of counseling, trauma, physical, mental, emotional, and spiritual exhaustion, it was time for dinner. I walked through the dining facility and found that I wasn't quite ready for all of the noise and laughter around me after such a somber day, so I took some tacos to go and headed for the roof of the hospital.

A million lights danced about the city. An occasional red

flare spontaneously erupted in the night sky, and I knew from experience that a plane had just deployed its flares. It was peaceful up there when all of a sudden a thick, ashen cloud engulfed me. Ash was in my eyes, stinging. It was also in my mouth, and I swallowed quite a bit before I could start coughing. My half-eaten tacos were grey.

I had to put my arms out in front of me and feel my way through the fog to get to the door leading back down into the stairwell.

On the first landing, I saw someone walking by staring at my ash-covered uniform, and I asked them, "Do you know where all of that ash just came from on top of the hospital?"

They covered their mouth and said, "You weren't up on the roof just now, were you? Every night at this time they burn all of the body parts in the incinerator behind the hospital. We just know not to be up on the roof when they do it."

Suddenly my mouth got extremely dry as I thought about how much ash I had just swallowed, and that's when I realized that I did indeed get to experience true alien cuisine after all.

It's a fact; I have an iron constitution when it comes to eating food. This isn't meant to be a boast, although I pride myself in the statement and boast about it often … Okay, it's a boast! I can eat just about anything and survive pretty much unscathed in the aftermath. That's why, when several members of my unit went to eat at a local alien restaurant with me some time ago and then complained of getting violently sick shortly afterward, I relished in the glory of my intestinal fortitude and ability to digest any harmful parasites as a bonus to the meal.

Conversations arose at the dining facility as these fellow soldiers finally began resurrecting from the dead about how miserable the experience had been for them. I lovingly invited them all to come back and eat at the restaurant with me again. Apparently, God wasn't amused.

The weekly message of hope I had been preparing to give happened to be in Daniel 4 when King Nebuchadnezzar looked out over Babylon and gloried at all he had accomplished and then was suddenly driven insane, forced away from civilization to eat grass like an animal and have his body wet with dew and start growing hair like feathers and his nails grow like the talons of an eagle until he would acknowledge God as being the Most High. I bring this up because something eerily similar happened to me.

I had left the dining facility, having sufficiently teased the weaker stomachs around me, and I went home to bed a happy, healthy man. I awoke the next morning seemingly underwater. My head was swimming. All heat had been sucked out of my room, and every inch of my body ached at the very thought of moving it. That's when I heard the strangest sound.

Do you know the sound the water dispensers make? The ones that have the big jug of water upside down with a spout to pour water into the little paper cones? It occasionally filters, and a big bubble rises up in it, and it makes a *blublublubloop* noise. Well, I heard that exact sound emanate from my stomach, and I knew the timer had just begun, and I had roughly thirty to forty-five seconds to dress, sprint down the hall, and locate an empty stall before Armageddon was upon me. I made it in fifteen because I bypassed dressing—it shaved off seconds on both ends—and I definitely needed the seconds for the back end.

I spent quality time thinking of the errors of my ways in a little stall in the middle of the desert on an alien planet erroneously named Hope, a planet that I am sure is an exact replica of where Nebuchadnezzar would have spent time thinking the same thoughts. Three courtesy flushes later, I looked at a shell of a face in the bathroom mirror and realized what dehydrated fruit must feel like. I made a valiant effort to dress and get out to do the daily routines of a chaplain, but it turned into a tourist visit of every port-a-john on Camp Cropper in a big circle arcing back to the barracks where I gave up and lay in the fetal position on my bed, shaking and burning up with fever for several hours.

At last I came up with a solution to my sickness, a way to be delivered from all my distress. It is an age-old remedy that has never failed me in fifteen years. I struggled into an upright position on the side of my bed and took a moment or two to convince myself of the necessity of going through with this. I swayed to my feet, shuffled in the dark to my computer, ripped it away from its cords instead of trying to individually undo them all, fell backward onto the bed, covered up with whatever cover was nearest to the position where I landed, turned on Skype, and told my wife I was sick and she needed to make it better.

She asked if I had taken any medication, and I said of course not. (This isn't because I'm tough, it's because I'm hopelessly dependent, and she wasn't there to give it to me. Sad, I know, but this is realty, folks.) After a rightly earned scolding, she demanded I ask for Ibuprofen or at least aspirin from someone. Fearing she would offer no further sympathy unless I agreed, I capitulated to her demands.

Two hours later, when I could bear the pain in my kidneys no longer, I made myself get up and stagger to the bathroom again. While there I looked over to my neighboring urinal user and asked casually if he had any medications he was willing to part with. Two Ibuprofens and one hour later found my fever broken and me sweating like I'd just finished a marathon. I checked myself for feathers—weird but fever-induced, I'm pretty sure.

The next morning at the dining facility, several fully recovered fellow Soldiers asked me if I was feeling okay, as I was looking pretty pale.

I knew I had to man up and say something to them since I had teased them all so much during their infirmaries, so I said, "I'm fine. It's just been so long since we've eaten at the alien restaurant that I'm weak from hunger. Do y'all want to go today?"

Despite this seeming relapse, when I prayed over my crackers (the only thing I could hold down), I acknowledged God a lot so He wouldn't feel the need to re-Nebuchadnezzar me again.

Veterans: Just because you can't see what
he's looking at...doesn't mean he can't.

I'VE SEEN SOLDIERS CRY

Many people have nightmares, but Soldiers tend to have memories, and often they equal the same thing. For instance, I am often scared by a recurring dream I have of Halloween, and it frightens me deep inside. Would you like me to tell you this scary story? It happened on Halloween night right before midnight, the witching hour. We had heard the haunting sounds of evening prayer eerily crying throughout the planet Mosul, just a few hours before sunset, but it was as quiet as the grave the hour that Death arrived at the CSH.

We were standing outside the ER in the dark. A blue strobe light was flashing on the worried faces of hospital staff awaiting casualties to scream around the corner. I'm sure there was noise, but I can't remember any. Just bodies lit blue then dark night, blue then dark night, blue then red strobes, green vehicles, dirty Soldiers, weapons everywhere, doors open, bodies hoisted out of the back—broken, bleeding, burnt, lifeless. They raced away from the vehicles, and Death slowly stepped out from behind them.

He was in no hurry. It was his night. He could smell fear, sadness, anger, and anguish. And as he strode past me and the other hospital workers in slow motion, we could smell him as well. The ER doors burst inward, and heroes were raced inside. The doors lingered in their swing, and Death walked in like a friend coming home. I was praying. Death didn't interrupt. Even he has someone to answer to. At the "amen," he took Captain Myers and Specialist Smith away from us.

We felt his sigh. I think even Death mourns the loss of Soldiers taken so early. What children did they leave unbirthed? What families did they leave unloved? What lives did they leave unlived? What memories did they never make? Like a gentleman, Death did not overstay. He appeared, an honor guard for warriors on a journey we will all embrace one day, and then he was gone. We will meet again. He brushed past us all, not in malice but with a gentle, "Not yet." I have met him before, but that night he hurt as we hurt, and I respect him more for it.

The bodies Death left were prepared like heroes of old resting high on their piers before being consumed in a burning glory. Draped in a symbol that binds us to a legacy of legends, two more legends took their places in the night sky. Fellow warriors left to continue the fight wept, pledged, honored, and said good-bye to their brothers in a dark little corner of a back room in a hospital that will forevermore be holy ground because of it.

SOLDIERS' TEARS

I've seen Soldiers who have been shot, blown up, and burned
Refuse to be treated until their buddies were seen to first.

I've seen Soldiers punctured, tired, hungry, spent
Smile at the sight of a pretty nurse offering a cup of water.

I've seen Soldiers roll up their dirty, blood-soaked sleeves
To give blood to slowly slipping-away insurgents
who shot at them hours before.

I've seen Soldiers with fragmentation ball
bearings protruding from their skin
Rotate in to give heart compressions to a
fallen brother and never miss a beat.

I've seen half-starved, beaten-down, sleep-
deprived, over-burdened Soldiers
Come alive and sprint to vehicles to respond
to a call for the fiercest of fights.

I've seen Soldiers scream warning to an entire
country that hell was coming
And am convinced that if only one went,
They would have won convincingly against any odds.

I have seen Soldiers who could not break, would not fall,
Who did not know or even begin to think of staying down.

I have seen Soldiers in a way the world has never seen them.
I have seen Soldiers cry.

Not because of the enemy, but *for* them.
Not because of their wounds, but because of
the wounds of their fellow Soldiers.
Not because of their pain, but because of the pain
to their children and spouses back home
Who must face birthdays, anniversaries,
and even deaths without them.

I have heard mortars explode to the sounds of Soldiers' laughter.
But I have heard tears that shattered my heart far worse
As they fall from the eyes of Soldiers.
Because they don't cry for themselves,
My tears must fall for them.

SYMPHONY OF TEARS, NOT OF REGRET

It had been a week full of sad times. I suppose it's appropriate then that I wrote this on the seventh of December, a day for sad memories in our nation. The week started out by receiving a call from another chaplain on post who asked if I would conduct a CISM for members of his unit. A CISM is a Critical Incident Stress Management session. You have those, obviously, after a critical incident of some kind. There in Iraq, the critical incident was almost always what it was in this case, the death of a Soldier.

I have led many of these discussion groups helping Soldiers work through some of the thoughts, emotions, and reactions they are experiencing after losing one that they care about and love. But I have never been to one that was easy or easily forgotten after its completion. This was no exception. I conducted a symphony of tears, hurts, and loss and led the musical score in such a way as to reveal the beauty of the music to the orchestra of hurting Soldiers. I left with the privilege of having heard the music and with the haunting sound of sadness that its notes played to my soul.

With words of advice and memories of my own listening ear fresh on my mind, I received news that my grandmother on my father's side was dying. I called her house and spoke with a man I did not know. He spoke kindly to me because he is my uncle. He is my uncle, and yet I did not know him. I experienced several different types of death that week, now that I think about it: the death of the Soldier and the ensuing grief of his friends. I did not know them, but I know grief, and I was able to comfort. Then I experienced the impending death of a good woman who I barely knew but loved, my grandmother.

That very same day I also spoke with my wife and heard that my close friend and brother Bill Colwell was struck by an IED. He was wounded badly and still had shrapnel in his brain. He was transferred to Germany for surgery, and his condition was critical. His wife would be flying up to Germany to see him, but due to the extent of the injuries, their children could not come.

As I write this particular paragraph it has been just over 10 years that people have been celebrating Bill's "Alive Day" after he was hit. He very nearly died and it took years and years to find even a semblance of new normalcy for his precious family. A portion of his brain actually had to be amputated. He had to relearn to read, write, walk and function all over again. With his wife and children at his side, however, he has proven every single day why Soldiers are so many people's heroes.

Although medically retired, Bill is still associated with a very elite group of Soldiers known as the Special Forces. These great Americans are known as Triple Volunteers, Quiet Professionals, and are quite literally the best Soldiers in the entire world. I just recently had the great privilege of meeting Bill's Command Sergeant Major that was with him on that terrible day. Command Sergeant Major Gary Beaver stood in the lobby of a hotel in downtown San Antonio, Texas as Bill and I walked in. I saw both men pause for half a heartbeat, chests swelled, jaws tightened, eyes glassed, and I realized they were no longer in the building. They were in Iraq, two Soldiers, each a decade younger. And then they were back. Noise flooded back into the room and they embraced as family. I was introduced and felt as if I had finally gotten to put a face to a family member I had heard spoken so highly of for years but had never actually met.

You can learn some important things about a person's character by what they say about someone in that person's presence. You can learn a lot more about a person's character by what they say about someone who is not in their presence. CSM Gary Beaver told Bill how much he cared about him and was glad to see him doing so well. He even asked about Janelle and the kids. I thought, "This man is really kind." It wasn't until Bill excused himself to go to the bathroom and the CSM said in a raspy whisper "When I saw the Black Hawk pull away with Bill on it I cried for three hours straight," that I thought, "This man is family."

A decade prior, when I first heard about the Black Hawk carrying Bill away to an unknown future, I cried for several hours straight. I was helpless. I could do nothing. I could offer no comfort. I could not rush to anyone's aid.

I strained to hear the words of advice and comfort I had just offered to others in order to apply them to myself, but the music of my painful heart drowned out any other sound. And so I smiled a smile that thinly masked the raging sea behind its calm façade. I left the laughter of other Soldiers to seek a quiet place to pour my soul onto paper. And I drew. I drew a picture of my friend, wounded and yet cradled in the loving arms of a gentle Savior that was there all along. And when I was done drawing, I wrote. And when I was done writing, I slept. When I was done sleeping, I got up, and I lived. I live to comfort those I can while I can. That is what I do because that is who I am. I am a chaplain.

FOR BILL

I am a Soldier.
And though I have fallen, I have not failed.
For I have had the courage to fight.

I am a son.
I am loved by my family, though war has
taken me far from their door.
I have fought for them
And I have won.

I am a husband.
I am married to an angel, who fights at my hospital bed.
She fights as hard as I have ever fought
To bring me love, hope, and a smile through
the hell she is enduring on my behalf
She is my hero.

I am a father.
My children are not ashamed of me.
I look in their eyes, and I see boys who wish to be men
To rush into hell on my behalf
And shoulder the fight I have turned over to others like myself.

I see a daughter's love that would raise me from
any injury to defend her again and again.
I am not fallen in my children's eyes.
If it is possible, I am raised even higher than
I have ever been in their hearts.
For I have fallen for them.

I am a Christian.
And though my body be wounded,
My soul and my spirit are strong.
My heavenly Father has walked the night with me in battle
And He has not left my side even now

I hear no rebuke in His voice as He sits with me,
Only pride, and love.
When I fell, it was He who caught me
And He who holds me still.

I am a Soldier.
And though I have fallen, I have not failed
For I have had the courage to fight.

THE FIRE

My Bible was in my office as it burned down. I have a lot of Bibles. I'm a chaplain. One Bible should be easily replaceable, but not that one …

May 16, 1999, I was standing in front of the congregation of Valley View Baptist Church in El Paso, Texas, with my wife, Jennifer, and children, Ashley and Kaylee. (Tina and Stephen hadn't been born yet.) The pastor, Brother Ron Fox, had just presented us to the church so that they could pray for us in our upcoming adventure. I was applying to enter the chaplaincy in the United States Army as a Soldier.

One of the requirements was that I be ordained as a minister of the Gospel by my denominational church. Valley View Baptist Church had been praying for us, encouraging us, and giving me opportunities to preach for over six weeks, ever since I first asked to be considered for ordination. On that day, the ceremony had just completed, and Pastor Ron Fox handed me a brand-new black Bible.

It fit perfectly in my hand as he told me, "Every preacher needs a good Bible."

On the first page was a handwritten note from the church reminding me that I was ordained to preach the Gospel.

I have carried that Bible with me ever since—from my acceptance into the chaplain candidate program; through years of seminary; and as a youth pastor, assistant pastor, and then as a chaplain in the United States Army. I had placed a picture of my family inside the front cover to remind me of the most precious things in my life.

My father-in-law, a master fisherman who has since gone to be with the Lord, took a fish hook and bent it over the front cover and told me, "Son, go be a fisher of men."

The eighteen long years since the Bible was first placed in my hands had worn its cover, torn its spine, which I have constantly taped back together, and loosened some of its pages, and I have to make sure they don't fall out when I carry it. It has weathered the hell of combat and brought care to the living, comfort to the dying, and honor to the dead. It has had its leather wet from the tears of the grieving and been sandwiched between me and the joyful hugs of the newly married. People who had lost hope found it rekindled in the pages of that beaten-up, black Bible that I carried with me everywhere.

At half-past midnight, there was a knock on my door. Knocks on the chaplain's door on war-torn planets at that time of night seldom came from bearers of good news.

I opened the door, and the First Sergeant said, "Chaplain, your office is burning down. The fire department is trying to put it out right now."

My office was one of three rooms in a long trailer beside the Veterans' Memorial Chapel. The two rooms next to my office were known affectionately to the Soldiers as the troop store. Packages of every shape and size got sent from patriotic Americans who love Soldiers, and they ended up in the troop store. Shaving cream, razors, ChapStick, candy, cookies, letters, envelopes, coffee, and a host of other goodies were sorted out and placed on shelves for Soldiers to come through and use. I ensured the doors were left unlocked twenty-four hours a day so that Soldiers working shift work could come whenever they got off work to get snacks and toiletries at their leisure. The fire started in the troop store. The fire chief believed it was something electrical, but it spread from the farthest troop store to the middle troop store to my office.

My Bible was in my office that burned down. I have a lot of Bibles. I'm a chaplain. One Bible should be easily replaceable, but not that one ...

The fireman exited out of the charred remains of the trailer covered in soot and said, "There's not much left in there. In fact, this was really all we saved." And he handed me a worn-out black Bible with a fishhook on the cover.

It was untouched. I wasn't.

WHY I BECAME A CHAPLAIN

Sergeant First Class Ford asked me, "Chaplain, did you hear we had several casualties and even a KIA?"

I had not. "No! Who was it?"

"Captain Terhark just came in and said she was at the hospital accompanying the detainee who is being treated when the call came in for a mass cal. At first it was like seventeen, then ten, then three. Two wounded and one KIA. She said she recognized them from Eagle Troop, the CAV guys."

"Does the BN commander know yet?"

"I'm not sure. She just came in and told me right before you got here."

Together we hurried to the BN Commander's office. As we opened the door, Sergeant Major Breckinridge was completing a brief to Lieutenant Colonel Nelson about the very event. We added the details shared by Captain Terhark, and I left with the Sergeant Major to get to the CSH to be with the Soldiers.

When we arrived, one Soldier was being wheeled past me into the CT scanner.

I placed my hand on his shoulder and said, "My name is Chaplain Dicks. I just want you to know I'm praying for you."

He reached up and took my hand. "Thank you, Chaplain."

And then they took him through the doors into the scanner.

The second patient was an interpreter. He had about six people around the bed getting his vitals, starting IVs, and checking his pain level. I put on a pair of gloves and took my position by his head where he could see and hear me without me getting in the way of the staff. I felt like I was back in '07 with the 28th Combat Support Hospital where I did this every day.

"Hello, my name is Chaplain Dicks. I want you to know I will be praying for you."

"Thank you, Chaplain."

"What is your name?"

"Joseph."

"Are you married, Joseph?"

"Divorced. I have a daughter."

"What is her name?"

"Maya."

The staff needed to take an X-ray of his swollen right arm, so I helped to lift it so they could slide the plates under it as he continued.

"I saw the Lieutenant get blown in half. They took him away in pieces," Joseph began, shaking with his tears.

I whispered, "We are happy you are still here, Joseph." And I placed my hand on his head and silently prayed for God's peace.

He stopped crying. "Do you know if anyone else survived?"

I answered, "Four of you were brought here, and the doctors just said all four of you are stable, which is good. Is there anything you would like me to tell them?"

"That I am okay, and see if they are all right."

The doctor asked if I could stabilize his head while they checked the rest of his body, which I did, and then I allowed myself to be crowded out of the way as the second soldier was being wheeled back in beside Joseph. I walked around the bed to get to his right ear where I could talk to him.

"Hello again, brother," I said as I placed my hand on his shoulder.

"What?" he yelled. "I'm sorry, sir. They blew my ears completely out."

Louder, I said, "I am Chaplain Dicks. How are you doing?"

"Oh, hello, Chaplain. I'm doing good, I suppose. I'm still alive. Do you know how the Lieutenant is? Is he here?"

"What we're concerned about right now is how you are."

"I'm doing okay. I've had better days. Been in the army seven years and finally got deployed. We were almost home. Then this happened. Is the First Sergeant all right?"

A doctor answered, "Your First Sergeant is in the CT scanner right now, but he's doing good and was wondering how you are."

"Tell him I'm okay."

"Where are you from?" I asked.

"Belton, Texas, Sir."

"I know it well. Any wife or kiddos?"

"No, Sir, I'm single."

"Well that's why the nurses were winking at you."

He laughed. As he did, I saw a large hole in his right side.

I whispered to the doctor next to me, "Has that been seen?"

He said, "Yes."

As they asked the Soldier to turn his head from side to side, I noticed a large hole in the back of his scalp.

I mentioned it to the doctor, and he asked, "Could you lift your head again, please?"

When he did, the doctor said, "Well, thank you, Chaplain. Nurse, could you get the stapler? We need to close this up." And they stapled his head closed.

The patient, Lieutenant John Flit, said, "Really? Staples?"

I told him, "We would have used thread, but with the draw down, all we have left is office supplies. It was staples or tacks. Which would you have preferred?"

He laughed again and said staples were good. I told him Joseph was right beside him.

His face lit up, and he turned to see Joseph. "You made it!"

They talked together for a while, and then I told them I would speak to them later and excused myself. Sergeant Major Breckinridge was outside, and we discussed the fact that they were not Soldiers from our Eagle Troop but a CAV unit from the smaller of Hope's two orbiting moons called Shocker. Their camp was scheduled to be shutdown the next day. They had been in a tent preparing for the camp closure ceremony when they were attacked.

We drove back to Camp Cropper to inform the command that the patients were stable and were not from our CAV unit. They had heard before we had. I walked back over to the S-2 office to let Sergeant First Class Ford know that I was back. We talked for a while and then together went to call it a night and head to the barracks.

As we were walking, Sergeant Major Breckinridge rounded the corner and said, "There you are, Chaplain. We need to go back. The hospital just called, and they are requesting you."

I told Sergeant First Class Ford goodnight, and we headed back onto Sather to get to the CSH and speak with whoever was requesting me.

When we arrived, a nurse directed me back to a darkened room where the interpreter, Joseph, was lying in a hospital bed.

"He's been asking for you. You can pull up a chair and sit by him."

I did just that. "How are you doing, brother?" I asked.

"I'm sorry I had to call you back."

I told him I was not sorry, that I felt honored he had called for me. "What's on your mind?"

"All night I have been seeing it. The Lieutenant blown in half. His name was Mitchell Adrian Noles. That is his full name. He was going to go back to the United States in just a few days and was so happy. I was happy, too, because he asked me to visit him, because I am going to the States too. He was a good man. So young." Tears were streaming down his face.

"I heard him screaming, but I couldn't believe it because he was in two halves. I swear to God I tried to get to him, but I was under Styrofoam and concrete. I had been by four t-walls. When I woke up, the t-walls were completely gone. I could not get his picture out of my mind. Tonight when you put your hand on my head, I felt peace for the first time, and I didn't see him anymore. I had to tell you that. I must tell you the truth. I have never believed in God. If God exists, and He is real, why would He let these bad things happen? Why would He let Lieutenant die like that? He was a good man. But tonight I felt peace when you prayed for me. Is God real? Can you tell me why He would let these bad things happen?"

I took a moment to consider his question and answered, "I believe God is real. And even though you have not believed in Him, He has always believed in you and loved you. God did not create evil, and it breaks His heart. It is His great compassion and mercy that holds back judgment for a time so that we may have the chance to receive His great forgiveness. He died to pay for the penalty of our sins, Joseph. He arose, conquering death to offer us life that we couldn't earn on our own."

"This is so comforting. It says on my birth certificate that I am

Muslim." He laughed while shaking his head. "I am not Muslim. I have never believed in Allah or the God of Christianity. I have a master's degree and have been a professor at a university for many years. I will receive my PhD in September."

"Congratulations," I said. "What was your thesis?"

"It was 'Why Was Nineteenth Century Iraq Not Influenced by Europe at All?'"

"What was your conclusion?"

"It is the three laws. In Iraq, you have the government law, the tribal law, and the religious law. If I walk down the street and want to spit, by government law it is okay. By religious law it is okay if no religious leader is near. By tribal law it is only okay if there is no Shake. We have so many laws that are so different, but many see them as though only one law. But it is so difficult there is no way we can keep it."

I nodded. "In the same way there is no way we, as human beings, can keep God's law. We are not good enough. We are sinners."

He shook his head. "Then there is no hope for me."

"There is good news, Joseph."

"What is the good news? You have said what I know. I cannot keep the law."

"The good news is that God has provided a way that we can be judged not by law but by His grace."

"How is this possible?"

He had a bottle of water sitting on the tray in front of him.

"Let us say this bottle of water cost five dollars. You don't have five dollars. I pay the five dollars for you and offer the water to you as a free gift. You could not afford it. You didn't have five dollars, but all you have to do for it to be yours is accept the free gift that I paid for on your behalf. In the same way, we cannot keep all three laws or three hundred laws or even one law. We are not good enough. God sent His Son, Jesus, to pay the penalty for our sins for us, to give us a free gift that we could not afford. All we have to do is accept that He paid for it on our behalf."

He placed his unbroken hand on his heart. "This God has done this for me? It says this somewhere? Do not lie to me, please."

I took the Manual for Hope from my ACU chest pocket and opened it to John 3:16. "For God so loved the world that He gave His one and only Son that whosoever believes in Him should not perish but have everlasting life."

"That is so wonderful," he whispered. "Can you teach me to pray to God?"

"I can teach you what Jesus taught His disciples when they asked Him that same question. Our Father ..."

He repeated after me every line of the Lord's Prayer while tears fell from his eyes.

When we finished, he said, "I want to be a Christian. What do I have to do? Do I need to wash myself before I pray? Do I need to pray every day? Go to church? I want to do whatever the Bible says to do for God to love me."

"Joseph, you have a daughter, don't you?"

When he said yes I continued, "What does she have to do for you to love her?"

"Nothing. I will love her no matter wh—" He paused and then looked at me. "Will God love me like this? No matter what? Like a child of His?"

I opened the manual to John 1. "He came to that which was His own, but His own did not receive Him. But to all who received Him He gave the right to become children of God. Children born not of natural descent or of a husband's will, but born of God."

"I want to receive Him," he said.

"Then ask Him to be your Father."

"Please, be my Father. Oh God, I have not believed in You, but tonight You have shown me Your peace. You have my life. I am Yours." After his prayer he asked if he could borrow a Bible.

I took out my pen and wrote in the front cover of my Bible, "To my brother, Joseph. May you always receive peace from the God who has always believed in you." And then I signed my name and the date and gave him the Bible as a gift.

Just then the First Sergeant was wheeled in

"Joseph! You're alive! Thank God!"

Thank you, God ... Thank you.

CONFIDENTIALLY SPEAKING, EVEN CHAPLAINS NEED HELP SOMETIMES

I remember when I was in Korea as a chaplain's assistant. The chaplain was gone (undoubtedly doing great things for God and country), and a young Soldier walked into the office. I informed the potential counselee that the chaplain was gone, and then I prepared to schedule a future appointment for him.

Instead he said, "I'll just talk to you."

I explained that I wasn't a chaplain and therefore was not authorized by the military to give official counseling advice. He said that was all right. He knew me from the unit and trusted what I had to say anyway, and he really needed help with his wife. She was constantly getting him in trouble with his chain of command. I asked what she was doing, and he told me.

"Each day she comes to the gate and demands that I come talk to her and start helping her pay rent."

"Your wife is Korean?" I asked.

"Yes." He went on to explain that they had only been married a few months.

"Don't you think it would be a good idea to help your wife pay rent?"

He nodded. "I would, but my wife back in the States won't let me."

I could make this stuff up, but it wouldn't be as creative. Throughout my years as a military chaplain, I have had the wonderful privilege of walking with Soldiers and family members through some of the happiest and saddest times in their lives. The journey has had incredible twists, turns, pitfalls, and surprises along the way, but it has been very worth it. My job in the midst of counseling is simple: instill hope. Listen attentively, hurt with the hurting, rejoice with the happy, be a friend, but ultimately it comes down to giving hope to those who desperately need it.

I could write a book solely on the various counseling sessions I have been a part of in my military career—each one filled with its own unique story of intrigue, mystery, deceit, passion, crime, jealousy, rage, hurt, laughter, and drama—a mini dime-store detective novel in each person or couple that have walked through my door.

The problem is chaplains have this thing called "absolute confidentiality." It means, like a Catholic priest who receives your confession, even a court of law can't get us to tell what was said in counseling … ever. It didn't used to be that way. Depending upon what religious denomination you were affiliated with, Catholic priests being a notable exception, there was normally a "duty to warn" clause in counseling sessions. This meant the chaplain was to inform his or her potential counselee before the session that if they began talking about wanting to harm themselves or others that the chaplain would have to inform the proper authorities to get them the help they needed to preserve life. This made sense to me.

Not everything that makes sense to me makes sense to everyone, however, so in 2007 the chief of chaplains issued a policy that was known as "absolute confidentiality." The policy removed the "duty to warn" clause and made it illegal to divulge anything regardless of the nature of the conversation to another party without the counselee's direct consent. Getting a blanket preconsent at the start of a counseling session was also prohibited.

After a lot of debate on the issue from multiple perspectives, the policy became chaplain law and revered almost as though it was one of the chaplain corps foundational beliefs. It became as quickly sacred as the noncombatant status of chaplains.

Some reading this may wonder about my own personal beliefs about the concept of absolute confidentiality and my belief about a chaplain's non-combatant status. I will put those questions to rest by saying my personal belief is "I will obey the orders of the President of the United States and the orders of the officers appointed over me according to regulations and the uniform code of military justice, so help me God."

Needless to say, absolute confidentiality makes it difficult to write about some of the most incredible stories I have ever heard. Not just of jaw-dropping issues in relationships, but of heart-wrenching heroism from Soldiers on the battlefield working through what their "new normal" looks like now that the world as they knew it has been turned upside down. I've listened to stories of battlefield action that Hollywood will never capture accurately, of PTSD earned from tender compassion toward those who had just tried to kill them. I have heard confessions of alternate lifestyles, of desire for death, of intent to commit murder, of crimes undiscovered, of undisclosed love, of newly discovered parenthood, of hopes and dreams for the future—and sometimes I have heard all of these in the same counseling session!

My job as a chaplain has placed me squarely on sacred ground in the lives of Soldiers and their families; it is a great privilege and a great responsibility that I have loved more than any other occupation I have ever attempted. I will one day receive separation orders from the United States Army and cease to be a chaplain, but I will never stop being a counselor to those in need. There is something about being on sacred ground in the lives of hurting people that is as healing for me as it is for them.

Being a chaplain has also given me a front-row seat to history. It's like having all of the perks of backstage passes to meet the actors and to get personal, one-on-one interviews for a commentary on the inner life and behind-the-scenes inspiration of the movers and shakers of our generation. To put it mildly, I chose well at the recruiter's office when I joined the military. Whether or not the military chose wisely with me will have to be determined by time.

Now, all of these incredible things that I can't tell you have done both good and bad things to my own character and the condition of my soul. I will try to explain what I mean. In Iraq, the combat stress control team had a therapy dog. Therapy dogs are incredible creatures. They are Soldiers just like I am and have their own rank. They always outrank their handler by one rank. If the handler is a Staff Sergeant, the therapy dog will be a Sergeant First Class. This way if a handler ever mistreats a therapy dog, they can be charged with assault on a Senior Non-Commissioned Officer.

Sergeant First Class Zack was the therapy dog I met in Al Asad—a playful, lovable, and relaxed yellow lab. As soon as I saw his wagging tail and smiling face (I think dogs can smile), I fell in love with him and instantly got down on the floor to play with him. He walked up to me, lay down, and placed his head in my lap so I could pet him. Every ounce of stress I had accumulated that day instantly disappeared. I was receiving unconditional love from a puppy who cared about me regardless of whether or not I had personality flaws, love handles, or bad breath.

That was Zach's entire job, caring for Soldiers. As I talked to the handler about Zach and other therapy dogs, I learned some very interesting things about their personalities. He said that dogs have the ability to sense emotion, and they take that emotion on themselves. During the aftermath of the Oklahoma City bombing, therapy dogs were used to identify which rescue workers needed to be rotated out. The dogs would search and find the most stressed-out workers and sit by them to love and be loved.

I was told that the dogs had to continually be given breaks. When I asked why, the handler explained that because they are so empathetic and compassionate, they absorb the feelings of the people they are around, and as a result, they end up getting extremely stressed. The handler said that Zach often got stressed and showed signs of fatigue and even depression after prolonged exposure to Soldiers who had been through traumatic events, and he needed breaks to recuperate.

As a chaplain, I have found that I relate a lot to Zach. All of the incredible things I'm not allowed to tell you can at times begin to accumulate on my own soul, and I begin, through caring so much for so long, to become compassion fatigued, overwhelmed, worn out emotionally, and become in dire need of a break. It is during these times that I rely heavily on the handful of family and friends that I have allowed to get close to my heart to comfort me and love me unconditionally. It's a tough job for them, because I am often needy at these times, but it's one that places them squarely on my soul's sacred ground and makes me forever endeared and indebted to them.

Provider, or providee, we all need a few Zachs in our life. They are the bringers of hope to drowning souls, and I have more than once been in danger of drowning.

"Your depression is onset by your surroundings."

Now that little tidbit of wisdom is not a clinical fact. It is instead a hand-scratched note on the door of the coed bathroom stall that was outside of my office; and seeing as how I was literally in the crapper when I read it, it made a lot of sense to me metaphorically.

It was nearing the nine-month mark on my second deployment to strange and exotic lands far, far away from home. Part of my job as a counselor and bringer of hope is to make sure my fellow Soldiers are taking appropriate care of their physical, mental, emotional, and spiritual needs while away from the earth they are used to. One of the dangers of this task, however, is that I can get so focused on making sure everyone else is getting the proper internal nourishment that I neglect to feed myself. It is what I have dubbed the Mother Teresa syndrome of starving oneself in order to feed the hungry.

Anyone can go for a few days without nourishment, just like treading water after having fallen out of a boat; you will be distressed but still be able to keep your own head above water. In a few weeks, it will become noticeable that you are becoming fatigued and taking in more water than normal, and after a few months, your drowning will be evident to all as you are no longer capable of coming up for air on your own. Before you actually drown, hopefully your inevitable splashing provides enough warning to your friends for them to come to your aid and lift you out of the deep water you're drowning in.

The smartest thing I have ever done is to find people that I respect, invest myself in them, and allow them the sacred privilege of seeing the "me" no one else is allowed to see. They get to know the human behind the uniform, the man behind the mask, the "seeker of help" behind the bringer of hope. The reason this is such an intelligent decision is because when all of my intelligence disappears and I go crazy, thrashing in an overwhelming sea of emotions that I have allowed myself to be overcome by one inattentive day at a time, they still care enough about me to collectively work to rescue my drowning self.

As a side note, it is an exhausting thing to rescue a drowning human being. I remember going to a lake in Arizona with my brother and his family. I was on an inner tube lazily floating in the center of this tiny lake with his daughter in her own inner tube not far away from me. Somehow she flipped over into the water and pushed her tube away from herself in her thrashing (which we all do in a metaphorical sense when we are drowning for some strange reason).

With my rescuer mentality, I flipped off my own inner tube and boldly swam to her to lift her back to safety. Instead of allowing me to save her, she kicked, pulled my hair, scratched my face, and clawed her way to the top of my body to get air, which in turn forced me under water to my own near distress. In fact, I had to swim away from her, decide she was still worth it, and then go around behind her to grab her and hoist her back into her inner tube.

My brother, who had been on the shore, having seen the scene unfold from a distance, had leapt in the water and was swimming toward us. By the time he reached us, it was all over and would have been regardless one way or the other because of how far away he had been.

I was exhausted, aching, scratched up, and half drowned after coming to her rescue and not very happy with her for having fallen out of the tube in the first place.

When we got to the shore, she hugged my neck and said, "Thank you, Uncle Stephen, for saving my life."

Suddenly all the aches and pains I had received were nothing in comparison. I knew I would do it over again if I had to because I cared that much about her.

In the same way, it is an exhausting thing to save a drowning person who has become overwhelmed with all of the various waves of life that continually wash over them. Investing yourself in people you care about makes it worth the hardship to save you. My heroes who laboriously asked me what was wrong, suffered with my sulking silence, brought me food I refused to eat, and lavished support on my seemingly ungrateful drowning self are Eddy Ford, Camille Acred, Sandra Chugen, and Teresa Watson. So I hug their necks with these words and say, "Thanks for saving me," on the days I almost drowned on a distant planet too far away from my family on earth to swim out to me.

GOING THE DISTANCE

Do you remember where you were September 11, 2001, the day the "aliens" invaded and attacked everything we knew as earth? I do. I was a youth pastor at a little church in Wichita Falls, Texas, working to help pay my bills while earning the required Master of Divinity degree I needed to get back into the army as a chaplain.

I say "back in the army" because I originally joined on July 3, 1996, one month after getting married to the love of my life. It only took that one month to realize we were going to be very, very hungry if I didn't get a job soon, so I joined as an Enlisted Soldier, a 71M Chaplain Assistant. By 1999, I had received a commission as a Second Lieutenant Chaplain Candidate in the Individual Ready Reserves and was discharged from the active duty Army to pursue the higher education requirements of becoming a chaplain.

On September 11, 2001, I had come home from the church to grab a bite to eat and saw my wife glued to the television set. There were the Twin Towers, one of them with plumes of smoke pouring out of the side. Terror had come to United States soil on a massive scale for the first time since Pearl Harbor, and I—like a majority of the shocked, angry patriotic Americans throughout the country—sat mesmerized, helpless to do anything else but watch.

It wasn't long before the second plane flew through the soul of Uncle Sam and ripped away thousands of more lives. I watched the towers crumble, one after the other, and prayed for all those trapped inside, at the base, and around the country who had just lost loved ones. Then I got extremely angry. Those were my brothers and my sisters who were just attacked, and I wasn't there to rescue them. I was angry with anyone who had so much as given a nod of approval to this horrible act.

I called my military branch manager and began pleading for the opportunity to be called to active duty early so that I could be a part of whatever counterstrike I knew would be coming shortly. I told him I was ready to deploy, just tell me where to report. He responded with a message that sounded as though he had said it a hundred times already that day (which he probably had). He told me this would be a long conflict, and the best thing I could do for my country would be to hurry and finish my degree and then come back in through the normal channels.

I still had three years left to finish my Master of Divinity degree! I knew if it came to war, it would be over long before that. The first time I remember America going to war, we had won before I could fill out an enlistment contract at the recruiter's office. So my older brother, Larry, who was already in the Army and had been since he was seventeen, went off to war in my place, and he gave 'em hell.

I threw myself into seminary and began taking ungodly amounts of semester hours to try and finish. It still took me three more years to achieve. By April 13, 2005, I pinned on my chaplain's cross and captain rank at Ft. Bragg, North Carolina. The two-star Chief of Chaplains, who happened to be at Ft. Bragg that day visiting the chaplains, pinned my cross on me, and

Jennifer pinned my Captain bars on me. The war was, surprisingly, still raging.

I was assigned to the mighty 28th Combat Support Hospital and in 2006 was sent on my first trip to a strange planet called Iraq. What was scheduled for a twelve-month deployment ended up getting extended to fifteen months. During this time, I became very familiar with the Soldiers' pain, suffering, heroism, and service to a country that had been at war since September of 2001. We as a nation had dug in our heels, set our jaws, and gone over to a foreign planet and were determined to go the distance, no matter how long it took, to bring the fight to whoever decided it was a good idea to sucker punch us back home on earth.

Going the distance in this particular war, and life in general, isn't about speed; it's about endurance. It is, in a metaphorical sense, not a sprint but a marathon. There are a lot of good life lessons that can be gleaned from running a marathon. None of which I could have hoped to understand, nor did I care to understand before that first deployment because I truly hate to run.

You see, I have this natural aversion to pain, and let's face it, running hurts! So I try to avoid it as often as possible. Having said that, on the first of November 2006, I did something I never thought I would do; I ran a marathon. A full-fledged 26.2 Twin Cities Marathon in the middle of Iraq. And somehow I'm still breathing in and out. Tell me there's no God now.

First of all, it took a miracle for me to sign up at all—at 1100 the night before the race. Way to train for a big run! But I was being hammered by Captain Rich Wood to join. He showed me this emotional video of a father who every year ran a marathon while pushing his disabled son. I told Captain Wood right off; he had convinced me, and as soon as he found a wheelchair to push me around in, I was as good as entered, but he wasn't buying it.

He explained to me that most marathons you have to pay to enter, fly to get to wherever they are happening, and then if you aren't fast enough, you aren't even allowed to finish. Yet being in an army marathon, the race comes to you. It's free, everyone gets a cool T-shirt and a medal, and there is no time limit. You could conceivably walk the entire way. That last one was the magical line for me. Walk the entire way. This was a once-in-a-lifetime opportunity to join a marathon and still not have to run. I let that saturate my brain until 1100 the night before the race. Then I signed up.

The next morning at 0530, I wasn't nervous at all. I had come to do what Captain Wood had said was conceivable. I had come to *walk* 26.2 miles. As soon as Rich Wood saw me, he came over and told me how proud he was of me—I was making a difference, I really cared, and this was the kind of chaplain he always wanted around him. In fact, he said he had decided to run the entire race right next to his chaplain who had made him so proud. Lucky me. I say again ... I *ran* a marathon. I had never done a full five-mile run. That day I did a ten miler, a half marathon, and a full marathon, all at once!

I also discovered it is physically possible to drown yourself while running. I found this out as we passed the first mile marker and saw cups with water and Gatorade set out for us to snatch as we ran by. Snatching it was easy. I even felt like a real runner, the kind you see on TV, for about half a second when I swooped that cup up without even breaking stride. But then I tried gulping down eight ounces of Gatorade in one splash while bounding up and down along the highway. Thankfully most of it shot back out due to a lovely thing called the gag reflex. Unfortunately, the rest of it just kind of rattled around in the middle of my throat for a while, making for cool gargling-slash-choking noises while I did my best to still try and look cool running. I think I pulled it off.

Rich ran with me for the first sixteen miles, and then he said, "All right, Chappy, you've already done everything you needed to do. You're on your own from here. The last ten miles is all heart anyway." And with that he sped up and disappeared, only to re-appear at the finish line an hour ahead of me.

The man's amazing, and very encouraging. So the last ten miles was just that, all heart. It had to be because no other part of my body was functioning properly anymore.

You know how, when you're swimming, the center of your foot cramps up and won't uncramp? That's the way both of my thighs and both of my calves were the entire ten miles I had left to finish.

At one point, an MP, who was slowly driving behind me to keep cars from running me over, pulled up beside me and asked, "Do your calves normally do that?"

I didn't have to look to know what he was talking about; because at that moment both of my calves were involuntarily spasming over and over again.

I looked wearily over at him and said, "Yes, sir, on every mar-athon I've ever run."

That satisfied him enough, so he slowed back down and con-tinued following.

Oh, what a feeling rounding that last corner was! What an inspiration it was to see that even though so many others had al-ready long since finished their races, they had stayed at the finish line to cheer me and the others behind me on as we finished.

There was Captain Wood yelling louder than all of them, "Way to go, Chappy!"

I'll tell you what, I am hard-pressed to think of any other time in my life when I have felt as much satisfaction and as much accomplishment as I did when I limped across that finish line. I had gone the distance.

I wrote this particular portion of my small part in American history ten years after the day I sat with my wife in front of a television set and watched my unmet fellow Americans die. And what And when I wrote, I was deployed once again to the planet Iraq as one more proof that America has the ability to go the distance to ensure we will never be hit with our guard down again.

The morning of August 31, 2011, Sergeant First Class Mitchel "Gunny" Vazquez from the 59th Military Police Company pulled me aside to tell me he had an idea. Gunny is called Gunny because of his prior service in the Marine Corps. His arms are covered with tattoos of the Memorial at Iwo Jima, and his trigger finger is tattooed with the phrase, "This is my safety." He served together with Sergeant First Class Ford at one point in history back on Planet Mosul and is yet another shining example of the best America has to offer.

He told me that starting at midnight September 1, 2011, he was going to have his Soldiers, and anyone who wanted to participate, begin running at the track on Al Asad. There would be a Soldier running at all times twenty-four hours a day for eleven days, finishing on September 11, 2011, on the ten-year anniversary of the reason we were there away from our families once again. The goal was to log at least 2,977 miles, one mile for every person who died in the twin towers. I was inspired. Once again I had the opportunity to prove to myself I could go the distance.

As a side note, I would encourage others not to think it is a good idea to wake up and decide to run a full marathon that same day unless you have been waking up that way for several months and training for it. Myself, I had all four wisdom teeth pulled at once because if I was going to have that much pain, I wanted it all over with at once. Seeing how people looked who had finished marathons they had trained for, I realized they didn't look much different from the way I looked when I finished the one I had not trained for. We all looked miserable; therefore, why would I want to be miserable training as well as racing? If I have to do it, I will do it once, and just get it over with. Again, I am often an idiot.

I got so excited about the run that I told my assistant, Specialist Thomas Nelson, that I was going to be at the opening ceremony that night and that I was going to try to run a full 26.2 mile marathon during this historic event Gunny was calling "A Run to Remember." Specialist Nelson unwisely decided his loyalty to me outweighed the intelligence of training and volunteered to run the race at my side as a chaplain and chaplain assistant Unit Ministry Team.

At midnight on the first, I said a prayer for all the runners, for the families of those who lost their lives a decade ago, and for all of the lives that have been forever changed as a result of that terrible day.

At the conclusion of the prayer, I said, "I would also like to introduce you to the Army's newest Captain."

First Lieutenant Justin Cox, the S-1 for our unit, called the small gathering of Soldiers to attention and recited by memory the orders promoting First Lieutenant Camille Acred to a Captain in the United States Army. Captain Acred's first official act as a Captain was to lead myself, Sergeant First Class Ford, Gunny, and the rest of us to the starting line where we began running in honor of those who died on September 11, 2001.

By the first lap, I had remembered I was an idiot, but that was all right because by the fifth lap I hurt so bad I couldn't even remember my name. Specialist Nelson, although much younger, much more physically in shape, and much faster, still made the conscious decision to slow his pace to mine so that we could run together. One mile, two miles, five miles, nine miles. Round and round the track we went. I told him that ten miles was the sexy mile because anything after ten just sounded cool to have run.

By mile eleven I was talking myself into stopping at a half marathon. My whole body ached. I wanted to quit. We had been running for literally hours. We were both tired and thoroughly miserable. Then I remembered sitting in my living room watching helplessly as the towers fell. I thought of police officers and firefighters who probably just wanted to go home but instead ran into the building instead of away from it to rescue people. It was mile sixteen before I felt sorry for myself again.

Specialist Nelson kept running ahead of me to get bottles of water or Gatorade. Then he would wait for me to catch up to him and let me get a drink. I would not have been able to make it without him as my battle buddy during the run. The one time I tried to slow my pace and bend over to snatch up the water bottle placed on the side of the track, both of my knees nearly gave way. By mile twenty, we were barely walking. We had not stopped our forward motion once throughout the entire night. Other runners had come, run, and left to be replaced by still others while we took one agonizing step after the other around the track.

At mile twenty-five, Gunny had returned to the track after a restful night's sleep and seen how far we had physically and mentally deteriorated, and he came to our rescue. He walked up next to us and cheered us on, telling us how proud he was that we were out here setting such a high bar for this memorial run, that we were going the distance.

With his encouragement, I got my second wind mentally. There was nothing left to recharge physically, and so I continued putting one bruised foot in front of the other. Twenty-six miles were finally completed with one victory lap remaining. Chief Chugan had come back to the track early that morning and was finishing her day's contribution to the run when she saw us. Standing at the finish line, she cheered as we finally completed the marathon of 26.25 miles in seven hours and fifteen minutes.

It was then we realized that we had walked the half-mile to the track from our rooms the night before and had no ride home.

Panic welled up inside me before Gunny said, "Don't worry about it, Chaplain. We'll have a squad car take you and Nelson home. I'm proud of you."

Over the next few days, I returned to the track several times to continue adding miles. Gunny made up his mind that at 4:00 p.m. on September 10, he would start running and not stop for twenty-four hours! He would finish the run at the concluding ceremony at 4:00 p.m. on September 11, which coincided with the time the second tower was hit in New York a decade prior. I ran the first three miles with him at 4:00 p.m. in the blazing sun and then wished him well. At 9:00 p.m. Sergeant First Class Ford and myself returned to the track and ran six miles with him as he completed his first marathon of 26.25 miles like Specialist Nelson and I had done. The only difference was he still had seventeen hours remaining. At 3:00 p.m. on September 11, 2011, I arrived back at the track in full ACU uniform. Gunny and his battle buddy Sergeant First Class Will were limping slowly around the track. They had just over two miles remaining to have completed a second marathon back to back—52.5 miles in one night!

I signed the logbook, "Captain Maria Ortiz's Mile," and then in full uniform and boots ran in the sun for an entire mile. I didn't see the track. I couldn't feel my labored breathing and didn't mind the stinging sweat in my eyes. All I could see was Captain Maria Ortiz standing in the hallway of the hospital in Baghdad in front of an American flag that had written on it "Freedom Isn't Free." She had a huge smile on her face like she always did.

I was in Mosul when I got called to the Commander's office. The Commander was crying. She never cried. When she saw me she hugged me and said she had just received a message from the hospital in Baghdad. There had been a mortar attack, and Maria had been critically injured. She was in surgery with her friends operating on her. The Commander Colonel Ruth Lee, the Deputy Commander Lieutenant Colonel Andy Lankowicz, and I joined hands and prayed our hearts out for a nurse we knew and loved, for a friend who cared so much for others. She died that night, and as we did her memorial service (Chaplain Major Pyo conducted the one in Baghdad, and I did the one in Mosul), the bulletin had her picture in front of that flag saying, "Freedom Isn't Free." The first nurse killed in combat since the Vietnam War.

The mile was over, it seems, before it even started. My uniform, drenched in sweat, hid the tears on my face. Sergeant First Class Ford completed a mile for Mason, the Soldier whose loss he felt so deeply, and logged it in the record book. His eyes were kind of sweaty too.

I said a prayer to begin the ceremony before Lieutenant Colonel Nelson spoke, followed by Command Sergeant Major Wallace, and finally Gunny, who limped up the stage to speak. Gunny told us that when he had originally thought of the idea for the Run to Remember, he had planned on only running 2,799 laps, one lap for every person who died in the two towers.

His squad leader said, "Too easy, Sergeant."

Gunny said, "I knew he was right. It was too easy, so I decided we would run 2,799 miles in just eleven days. It seemed impossible at the time, but when we told the Soldiers what the run was for, we actually reached that goal within the first forty-eight hours.

So I decided to change the goal again—one mile for every life lost since 9/11 to include those who died in the towers; at the Pentagon; in the field in West Virgina; and in OIF, OEF, and OND—9,191 lives, 9,191 miles. I have just received the total miles we've run in the last eleven days—10,513 miles."

I'm proud of Gunny, of Nelson, of Captain Acred, of Sergeant First Class Ford, of Chief Chugan, of Master Sergeant Watson, of thousands upon thousands of Soldiers, Civilians, and Family members who have faithfully continued to put one aching foot after the other for the last sixteen years of a prolonged war. They are my heroes. They are the ones who have gone the distance.

SSON, Adam SPC	59TH MP	0700
l, Brandon SFC	54TH MP	1100
LE, DONALD SFC	40th MI BN	1200
orton, AAhv	407th	1350
Segura, Michael	Aco 2B35TB 82m	1411
STEPHEN DICKS	"Maria Ortiz's Mile"	1500
J MAJ	USF-I J5	1520
	HORN	
d	Casey Masons mile	

SAYING HELLO AND GOOD-BYE

"**A**nd there shall be wars and rumors of wars ..." There have been wars and rumors of wars almost from the instant Jesus first uttered these words. So ... are these wars and rumors of the same any different? Our old men are dreaming dreams. Our young men are having visions. The Holy Spirit is poured out on all flesh, and the Gospel is proclaimed throughout all the earth. Peter may be officially cleared from any possible accusations of being a false prophet. What he said through the Holy Spirit has come to pass. Are we then finally in the last days?

Well, one thing is for sure; these are the last days for everyone currently on the earth. The furthest stretch one can hope for a lifespan is about another one hundred and twenty years for the rarest of us. For everyone else the sand is slipping far faster through the hourglass, and our day of judgment looms ever closer, rushing toward us at an alarming pace.

I don't say this to be morbid or to incite panic. I'm only stating the obvious. Each of us has been destined a time to be born, live, and die. Today, we are one day closer to our moment before the Eternal Judge, for the vassal to meet the Master, the subject to see the King, the condemned to hear his acquittal or condemnation. These are our last days.

I am a chaplain in the United States Army, a missionary to the military. Instead of liturgical robes or a suit and tie, I wear tan combat boots and a digitized uniform designed to help me blend into my surroundings. My personal goal, however, is not to blend but rather to shine a light in a dark war while working among the warriors of our nation.

Please understand when I say we are engaged in a dark war. I am not making any political statement about a just war or fighting for a righteous cause. I am once again only stating the obvious. War is a dark thing filled with violence, sadness, and death. It is upon this mission field that my boots walk each day. The valley of the shadow of death is my pastoral office, and yes, Jesus is alive and well, actively rescuing eternal souls even here ...

I sat in the ancient ruins of a house in Tallil, Iraq, the modern name for the city of Ur. This particular house was stamped with cuneiform inscriptions claiming that it belonged to Terah, father of Abram, Nahor, and Haran. With a small group of dusty Soldiers huddled together, the sand whistling through the ancient archways, I preached about God's call for Abraham to leave that very spot and to go to a land He would show him.

God's call was to leave the wealth, splendor, and idolatry of Ur to follow by faith the one true God. The invitation was then given for the Soldiers to leave their own personal idols behind in the ancient ruins of Ur. There in Iraq many thousands of years after God's initial call to Abraham, God called the hearts of several Soldiers to follow Him, and as they walked out of Ur, they too received new names, that of Christians.

Sitting on top of a hill on the east side of the ancient city of Nineveh, I sat with an open Bible amidst another group of Soldiers. Together we read the book of Jonah, and I smiled as I heard gasps of recognition when we came to the point where the Prophet Jonah sat on a hilltop on the east side of the city of Nineveh and wondered why God had sent him to such a wicked people.

In Jonah's mind, they were all sinners and needed annihilating, but God responded, "Shouldn't I care for this city with all of its inhabitants who don't know their right hands from their left?" (Jonah 4:11, NIV). Jonah never answered. The question was left dangling throughout the misty ages of time, flung thousands of years into the future to once again be posed to a group of battle-weary, compassion-fatigued Soldiers sitting roughly in the same spot as when God first asked the question.

Mortars had ripped through the Green Zone in Baghdad, Iraq. One of the things it hit was a swimming pool by the gymnasium that I had hoped to use as a baptismal pool. Looking for an alternative, I found that Saddam Hussein had a very luxurious swimming pool at his palace, a palace now occupied by allied forces.

Leading a group of Soldiers in their PTs, we gathered along the edge of a pool in the inner courtyard of a palace once belonging to a Muslim dictator. I stepped into frigid waters and preached the Gospel clear and plain then had the privilege of baptizing a newly won-to-Christ soul in the name of the Father and of the Son and of the Holy Spirit.

These are our end times. Christ comes at His appointed hour and shall not be late. We are closer at this moment than any human being has ever been to the bodily return of Christ the eternal King. These are our last days. Expect the harvest God can bring by using every single moment we have left for His glory.

"Behold the fields are white unto harvest, but the laborers are few" (Matthew 9:27, NIV). In these last days, despite what may be seen on CNN, God is reaping a great harvest in modern times among US Soldiers even as He did in the ancient land of the Bible, and I have been given the privilege of a front-row seat to watch Him acting in history.

Despite the moaning and groaning of Soldiers who are always talking about when they get to go home and leave whatever current hell hole they're in firmly in the past, there is still a sense of sadness that comes with the ending of a combat mission.

Entire conflicts have been fought over and decided by politicians on battlefields of paper and podiums that I would never want to be a part of. The conclusion? At some point they say "The troops are tired, and it's time to close this chapter of America's glorious military exploits." By "the troops are tired," I mean that the civilian population has grown tired of an extended war, sending their children off to become hardened shells of their former selves. Ghosts still somehow wrapped in flesh. Any war is expensive. A war lasting well over a decade is unimaginably so. Soldiers are always tired, but they still do their jobs. It's when everyone else who doesn't actually fight the wars get tired that enough is finally enough.

Normally at the conclusion of a twelve-to-fifteen month combat mission, the unit will collectively fly back from whatever foreign planet they've been on to their earth as a team to the roar of applause and tears and happy smiles from family and friends who have been waiting for countless hours for their Soldiers to return. I remember the first time I redeployed like it was yesterday.

The whole plane cheered when we heard the pilot over the intercom saying, "Welcome back to the United States!"

Oh, the visions I had in my head of walking off that plane in formation with my maroon Airborne beret and combat patch on my right shoulder, hearing the families yell and cheer and applaud as we marched in crisp formation, executing a sharp left face inside of the Green Ramp Bay. Facing right in front of me would be my children, all smiles and proud that their father had returned home. Arms would be outstretched. They would run to me, and I would hold them forever!

"Flight attendants, prepare the plane for landing!"

This was it. Fifteen months of deployment for this reunion! Taxi to a stop. Everyone on their feet. Berets in place, a badge of honor in itself. Check each other's uniform, looking sharp. Exit the plane. Crisp cold attacked my body, and I felt alive! It wrapped around me, causing my heart to race, or was it the anticipation?

The Green Ramp Bay doors were open, and I could already hear a muffled roar from the inside, though it was off in the distance. In formation. Boots clicked, left, right, left, right, left, right. Moving as one. I love the army. Then suddenly, like a crash of a tidal wave onto the shore, the band began playing, and hundreds of voices were cheering, and the roar of the applause had never been this loud during a parade in Times Square, and I was surprised to find myself holding back tears that had welled up from nowhere.

"Mark time, march! Group, halt! Left face!"

One swift motion, like one Soldier.

I couldn't believe it! Right there in front of me, sure enough, were my children! Stevie was holding a sign that said, "I love you, Daddy!" Kaylee was smiling and waving so hard I knew her arm was going to be hurting later. There was Tina smiling, and on the bench step above her, her big sister, Ashley, tears in her eyes, choked up because Dad was home!

I didn't think reunions were actually supposed to happen like you imagined them. I thought all of the presentations said you shouldn't get disappointed because reunions seldom live up to the fantasies you have about them. Yet there I was. It was exactly like I had dreamed it would be. This was it!

And then Ashley threw up right on top of Tina's head, spilling puke down into her hair, causing her to sympathy puke into the crowd in response while looking up at her big sister with a "Are you freaking kidding me?" look of betrayal in her soggy face. Jennifer, seeing what had happened, was trying to rush in to rescue her sick little angels but kept getting elbowed back by people thinking she was just trying to get a better spot in line. And so the sweet world of reality rushed back to me, and I was glad. The real stuff has always been a lot more fun to live than the fantasies anyway.

Even that return trip, however, had its bittersweet moments. Family members and fiancés of Soldiers we had taken with us fifteen months prior but who had died in combat still came to see the rest of us home. It tempered our joy with a pain that always resides within the heart of combat veterans. Every dining facility and formal military function has its solitary table set up in remembrance of the captured, missing, or fallen among our ranks that cannot be with us as we celebrate. It honors those we cannot, must not ever forget.

Those who were forged into family by the most extreme circumstances life can offer slowly fade away from each other on different adventures down different roads that life marks out for them. Some to lay down the weapons of war and hang uniforms in the back of closets only to be seen on special occasions or when nostalgia grips tightly on hearts longing for specters of friends who shared horrors no one else could ever understand. Some to other units to relearn the art of relationship building with those whose only common ground are souls longing for those too soon left behind. There are always new memories to be made and old stories to be told to fresh ears and ever-widening eyes.

Every so often diverged roads reconnect in their twists and turns, and faces once so familiar are seen again in a different setting, and the past comes to life with all its glory, and forgiveness is granted for mutual embellishments of events that finally bear two living witnesses. Each face re-found is a precious treasure often remembered.

I've discovered as Soldiers begin to age, these memorable few have become so dear and so immortal in stories so often told that new relationships stand little chance at measuring up. As a result the new relationships are often inadvertently sabotaged at every stage until like a self- fulfilling prophecy they do not stand the test of time. They don't measure up to the faithful and steadfast heroes once served with, ones who would never dream of leaving a comrade in arms. In fact, saying hello becomes harder and harder as the years go by, because for a Soldier, "hello" always leads to an inevitable and painful good-bye.

My second deployment saw several smaller good-byes, like trial runs for the final test. There was a large surge of units and Soldiers pouring into Al Asad Air Base from all over the country looking for their exit visas and return trips to the States and to families and loved ones that had been waiting anxiously for over a year for their return. The PX was bombarded with buyers looking for final purchases of everything from chips to souvenirs. Chocolate was a myth often spoken about but rarely seen.

Sergeant First Class Ford shared his wise philosophy with me one day as we stared rather disgustedly at all too barren shelves in what was left of the PX. "I say, if you're going to eat it in the States, don't buy it in Iraq."

Translated, he was saying what we all felt: "Y'all are going home where this stuff is readily available. Leave it for us unfortunates that still have time to serve."

Then one day, suddenly, it was just us. All the other units met their flights and moved out in smart military fashion, and we were left to watch the tumbleweeds drift lazily over the now-barren streets. It felt like we were in a movie of a post-holocaust city. The same buildings were there, but now everything was empty and silent.

The post office set a deadline for incoming mail, and just like that, all of the goodie packages from home giving us a respite from repetitious DFAC food ceased coming in. Soldiers began trading goods like school children with lunches their parents had packed for them.

"I'll trade you a ramen noodles for a can of Wolf Brand Chili."

Not long after that, the post office closed its doors to even outgoing packages. Whatever was left would be left or carried on our backs back home. The big blow came when even the DFAC closed its doors for the last time. The line stretched for hours to get in for that last meal. For many Soldiers unable to handle long lines, whatever meal they had eaten prior to this one became their last DFAC experience. I was in that crowd. Ramen noodles and a bottle of water marked the day the dining facility closed for me. The problem was Thanksgiving was still a week away, and now it looked to be a three MRE (Meal-Ready-to-Eat) celebration for everyone.

MREs have greatly improved since I entered the military some twenty-plus years ago, but at the end of the day, it's still a sack lunch. Thanksgiving with no post office, no gym, and no turkey was looking like it was going to be one punch in the morale after the other. I didn't know that Jennifer was back home heartsick at the thought of her Soldier not getting to eat a real Thanksgiving dinner on Thanksgiving.

She had all the spouses at PWOC (Protestant Women Of the Chapel) and all of the members of her Sunday school praying that God would grant a miracle and feed her hungry man in the desert. I have read the story in the Bible of how God miraculously allowed quail to come out of seemingly nowhere in the desert to feed a hungry and grumbling group of Israelites, but this Thanksgiving I got to experience the power of a praying wife and see with my own two eyes that God can still do anything He wants.

Resigned to a sack lunch with grumpy friends, I looked up and saw a smiling Sergeant First Class Gunny Vazquez.

"What's with the big smile, Gunny?"

"Chaplain," he explained with a big grin, "I'm here to make your day. The Special Forces just pulled out of their compound and left me the keys to their milvans."

I wasn't exactly sure where this was going. "What was in them?"

His smile grew even bigger as he answered, "Food! Lots and lots and lots of food! Turkeys, chickens, pizzas, hot pockets, beans, steaks, anything you can imagine. Enough for everyone. We're having Thanksgiving dinner!"

I couldn't believe it. I had accepted that it would be a sad routine day on Thanksgiving. Instead it turned out to be a great filled-with-laughter, barbeque-beans, turkey, stuffing, dressing, cranberry-sauce, sparkling-grape-juice-in-champagne-bottles, and friends-with-immortal-smiles-that-could-not-be-wiped-away kind of day that I will always remember.

When I spoke to my wife, Jennifer, that night on Skype, I couldn't even finish telling her all that I had stuffed myself with before she began sobbing with joy and gratitude for a God who once again, miraculously fed meat to a grumbling, hungry people in the desert.

Good-byes came one at a time at first to this or that Soldier I had befriended through chapel or the various gym-related programs. Then they came in mass as everyone seemed to be disappearing at once. Finally it was our time.

We said good-bye to the office we had been working in for the past six months. Taking down the drawings that covered my office wall and turning off the lights for the last time, we said good-bye to the post office, gym, Green Beans coffee house, the dining facility, and at long last to the detainees at the prison.

I went with Sergeant First Class Ford to his office at the now eerily silent facility whose hallways echoed with every step we took. Doors were locked, gates were closed, and a chapter was finally written in history.

The detainees were all transferred back to the government of Iraq with the exception of a small minority of high interest people that we needed to hold on to until the last possible moment. To do so meant moving them to another secure location in Iraq and separating our 40th MP family right at the finish line. It was with a strange mixture of joy and sadness we shook hands, hugged, prayed for, and slowly tore ourselves away from fifteen of our brothers and sisters in arms that were chosen to remain behind for an undisclosed amount of time with the remaining detainees. That was a difficult good-bye for each of us to say.

We landed at Forbes Field and were bussed back to Fort Leavenworth with an honor guard of motorcyclists in the front and back. It was a presidential welcome from an honor guard of grateful Americans. Vehicles honked, and little children waved from the backseats of cars, respectfully pulling to the side for us to hurry home to our families. The streets of Leavenworth were lined with cheering people.

We left the bus on a crisp December day and marched to

the closed doors of the gym, where our most precious treasures were waiting inside for us. Captain Shayne Estes, the Company Commander for HHC 40th MP Battalion, banged three times on the metal door, and an eruption of cheers and applause struck my heart like a hammer as I fought back tears of pride and joy that assaulted me from out of nowhere.

The doors slid open to waving flags, crying spouses, and jumping children, screaming and pointing with joy for their mommies and daddies in uniform.

"Left, right. Left, right. Left, right. Mark time, march! Group, halt! Left face! At ease!"

Thunder rolled with rounds of applause. A sea of faces suddenly faded when my wife and children's teary smiles came into focus.

Everyone in the room disappeared except for them. My chest swelled even farther than it had been, so much that it hurt, but I didn't care. I was home. Speeches made, prayers said for those left to return, handshakes on a direct line to embracing arms that enveloped me like a flood and gripped me like a vice I never wanted to loosen.

Saying hello instantly meant saying good-bye to others we had held so close for the past year. Those who substituted for a listening ear and friendly companion were forced to the side of our thoughts for the ones we had given our lives daily to return to. We were home, yet in the days to come, we would not be able to avoid the nagging feeling that somehow, even surrounded by the ones we had so dearly longed to reunite with, we were, in some ways, home alone.

I complete this writing now, safely at home with those I love, but every now and then, I find myself secretly hoping for orders to deploy once again. Don't get me wrong. There is something nice about being surrounded by all of the familiar settings of home, wife, children, pets, friends, and places soaked with memories only you know about. I call this environment "life on earth." And life on earth is great, but maybe that's part of the problem. For a Soldier who has become accustomed to being torn away from his or her "earth" and sent to war on what seems to be an entirely different planet, everyday life on an otherwise great earth can sometimes become a little too great to handle.

"Et Spes Infracta." And Yet My Hope Is Unbroken.
Motto on the Dicks' family crest.

Chaplain Dicks is a Soldier, a Chaplain, a Husband, and a Father of four children. He is best known for his cartoon series "Another Monday." A series of military cartoons published on a weekly basis in multiple newspapers throughout the country to include the *Fort Bliss Monitor*, *The Fort Bragg Paraglide*, *The Ingleside Index*, *The Fort Leavenworth Lamp*, *The Dugway Dispatch*, and *The Fort Hood Sentinel*.

Also included in his writings are; *"Journaling as a Means to Spiritual Renewal (Help for the Compassion Fatigued)"*. A dissertation submitted to the faculty of Erskine Theological Seminary for the Doctor of Ministry Degree May 2009: approved by the examining committee and accepted by Dr. Lloyd Melton, the Director, Doctor of Ministry. It can be found in the McCain Library at Erskine Theological Seminary in Due West, South Carolina. Also "Spiritual Thoughts From the Front Lines," an article published in the internationally circulated magazine, *The Lamplighter*, in the January-February 2010 edition.

His extended military career has spanned over 20 years beginning as an Enlisted Soldier, transitioning to a Commissioned Officer in the Individual Ready Reserves, and then has continued on into the present day with his service as an Active Duty Army Chaplain who councils Soldiers daily. This journey gives him a unique insight into the daily lives of Soldiers that is reflected in his writing. His Military Awards reflect a mastery of both his highly specialized ministerial skills and his successful application of military knowledge of what it takes to be a Soldier and a Leader. This foundation gives him an ability to write with an insight that others find informative as well as entertaining.

Military Career

1996-1999 US Army Chaplain Assistant (Specialist), Tong Du Chon, S. Korea, Ft. Bliss TX.

1999-2005 US Army Chaplain Candidate (First Lieutenant), Ft. Bliss, TX, Ft. Sam Houston, TX, Ft. Bragg, NC.

2005-2013 Us Army Chaplain (Captain), Ft. Bragg NC, Iraq, Ft. Sam Houston, TX, Ft. Leavenworth, KS, Iraq, Ft. Jackson, SC, Dugway Proving Ground, UT.

2013-Present (Major), Ft. Sam Houston, TX, Ft. Hood, TX, Ft. Sam Houston, TX, Ft. Eustis, VA.

Military Awards

The Bronze Star Medal
2 Meritorious Service Medals
2 Army Commendation Medals
5 Army Achievement Medals
The Meritorious Unit Citation
The Army Good Conduct Medal
The National Defense Service Medal
3 Iraqi Campaign Medals for Combat Service
The Korean Defense Service Medal
The Army Service Ribbon
2 Overseas Service Ribbons
The German Efficiency Badge

Printed in the United States
By Bookmasters